FUNKYTOWNS
USA

the best alternative, eclectic, irreverent and visionary places

BY
MARK CRAMER

A meticulous effort was made to assure that all locales mentioned in this book were still in existence at the time of completion of the manuscript. Nevertheless, the nature of contemporary business makes it inevitable that one or two of the restaurants, hotels or personalities mentioned will have gone out of business, changed location or vanished.

The author would like to thank the many people who helped with this project, either for providing perceptive information, reading sections of the manuscript or setting him up with a comfortable place to work while on the road, especially Gary McMillan, Martha Cramer, Bronwyn Belling, Bill Olmsted, Winchell Dillenbech. Phil Buterbaugh, Reggie Soileau, Jim Stewart, Amy Harper, Susan Kern, Debbie Nathan, Father Michael Guglielmelli, Michael James, Rick Auerbach, Mike Helm, Marcus and Gordon (from San Francisco), Kara Keskitalo Larson, Bill Bracco, Celeste (from Ward), Bernd Zimmerman, Bob Owens, James (from Burlington), Beth and Bob (from New Orleans), Felicia Harper, Fred and Tanya, Bruce and Leslie, Edgard and Maureen, Frank and Kris, his Aunt Ada, Jason Davis, Siomara, Morey and Ouida, Mary Jo Thorne, Dick Carter, Bob Fellows, Karen Starr and too many others to mention here, including the written sources of information who are thanked by way of the bibliography at the end of the book.

TBS PUBLISHING
P.O. Box 6283
Annapolis, Maryland 21401

Library of Congress Catalog Card Number: 95-90413

Design and Layout by Blue Moon Graphics, Inc.
Printed in the United States of America

Library of Congress Cataloging-in-Publication Data
Cramer, Mark 1945 -
    FunkyTowns USA: the best alternative, eclectic, irreverent and visionary places / Mark Cramer

    1. Travel—United States 2. Alternative Culture

ISBN: 0-9646815-0-1

10 9 8 7 6 5 4 3 2 1

for my children
Marcus, Siomara, Monty, Gabriela and Vivi,
each of whom will appreciate the places in this book
for their own reasons

*"...this city, closing its doors,
barricaded, almost empty,
mournful without tears..."*
—Charles Bukowski

TABLE OF CONTENTS

FOREWORD

PREFACE

INTRODUCTION

PLACES EVALUATED

ALSO-ELIGIBLE PLACES

FINAL TALLIES

BIBLIOGRAPHY

PRIMARY INFORMATION INDEX

FOREWORD

Sometimes, in the milltowns, the wind changes and a sweetness of lilacs replaces the noisome issue of the smokestacks. In like manner Mark Cramer's *FunkyTowns USA* affords redolent relief from the statistical fetor of those "places rated" books which have become their own genre within the past decade. Against the blurred blandness resulting from the wholesale averaging of secondary data, Cramer's places stand out in sharp, enticing relief. Here are identified unique and authentic places preserved against the copycat zoning ordinances and corporate cloning that have made most of America a traveler's monotony.

Accordingly, there are no statistical tables to interrupt the rich descriptions of fifty-five locales the author has discovered in thirty of our United States. Twelve criteria are employed in the rating of "funky places," all of which bespeak the unusual and unconventional, none of which are found in the tabular treatments. Among the dozen indicators, unconventional local customs, successful cultural diversity, and local variation in climate or geography are given top weight. Mixed land use, pedestrian friendly streets, and genius in converting old buildings to new uses garner slightly fewer points as do alternate economies and a history of independence in politics.

How does one use this volume? The author suggests that these places should be considered for vacations, for retirement, and as places to raise children. Though he doesn't warn against quick side trips or half-day visits, his descriptions suggest that much too much would be missed in a brief stop at some of these locales—it takes a bit longer to appreciate a way of life than to appreciate the Grand Canyon.

The book has value beyond its use as a guide, as well. It is a lesson in planning and preserving human habitat in a society that needs, urgently, to learn how to do just that. Many a municipality and its citizens may discover much, here, about how to achieve a sense of place, how to humanize a town or a neighborhood against the utilitarian excesses which have rendered community moribund.

And finally, the book is superb entertainment for the armchair traveler. What delight to read about places where guests are put up in tree houses, where an All-Species parade is an annual event, or about the little Minnesota town where entrants are invited to compete in the annual "Great American Think-off."

My hope, and it is a reasonable one, is that some wonderful American undiscovered places will resent their omission and eloquently plead for inclusion in a revised edition. Whatever encouragement we can give our all-too-rare connoisseurs of places will surely enrich us all.

RAY OLDENBURG, author of *The Great Good Place: cafés, coffee shops, community centers, beauty parlors, bars, hangouts and how they get you through the day.*

PREFACE

Statistics don't lie, they deceive. Rating places on the basis of average this and average that leads to average places. Right now in the United States of America (USA), the mainstream type of place is characterized by alienating suburban sprawl or dehumanizing urban renewal. There is much sameness across this land.

This monoculturalism has arisen as regional shopping malls drive Main Street USA out of business, the iconization of the automobile destroys pedestrian life and public transportation, single-use zoning breeds "communities" with only one dimension, and the corporate media irons out all the interesting creases in our cultural landscape, leaving us with a flat, one-dimensional world view with few alternatives. What totalitarians attempted to do with an iron fist in other countries is being done softly and quietly to the USA as a result of our blind utilitarianism.

Yet, there are inherent characteristics of the United States that resist this homogenization. We are a nation of immigrants, who carve out a profusion of alternative pathways. Various cultures that survived the abuse of conquest and slavery have contributed to this diversity. Our constitution, born out of a revolution, in many ways encourages rebelliousness and defiance.

All across the nation, there are places that refuse to accept the mainstream way of doing things. The word *funky* is a metaphor for unconventional, bluesy, bizarre, eclectic, iconoclastic, or simply alternative.

FunkyTowns USA uses a revolutionary methodology of rating places, based on their originality. Find the place where children are dismissed from school to help with the potato harvest, the town where the owner of the local brothel is also the sponsor of the little league, the city that defied both Democrats and Republicans by electing an independent congressman, the neighborhood where old factories have been converted into apartments, the places where you can change your climate from hot to cold, and back, in a matter of minutes, the city where there are no property taxes and public transportation is free, the place that gets its identity from the man who burned it down, the town where the prevailing wisdom demands the use of outhouses instead of toilets, the place labeled a "culinary Woodstock," the town where the blues has survived in its original juke-joint habitat, the city where two very different nations dynamically interact.

These are but a few of the many unconventional traits of the funkiest places in the USA.

Are you looking for a great vacation? Why choose a theme park that imitates uniqueness when you can visit authentic places that theme parks try to copy?

Looking for a retirement location? Before you choose bland Condominiumville, check out these places where every day is a new adventure.

Simply looking for a place to raise your children? You may find just the right spot here, one that will nurture your kids' natural originality and protect them from being homogenized into the monoculture.

FunkyTowns USA celebrates the countercurrents that make this country much greater than it would have been had the settlers at Plymouth Rock had it all their own way.

INTRODUCTION

FunkyTowns USA offers an alternative to a growing number of books that attempt to rate the quality of life of large and small cities, based on misleading statistics.

The first of these books, *Places Rated Almanac* (1985), set the statistical standard for the genre. Without diminishing the value of these studies, their dependency on number-crunching leads them on the road to Everywhere, USA, often bypassing cities and towns with a truly unique sense of place.

City-wide statistics are especially misleading. Cities are divided into neighborhoods. Some neighborhoods have personality, others are dull and colorless. Some are marked by a high level of tolerance and solidarity while others have no sense of community and are intolerant. Surely, when analyzing the value of a place, that place must first be delineated by more than a broad-brush average.

When crossing this country, stopping off to visit or live in places along the way, all too often one finds a void, a strip-mall, fast-food, suburbanoid sameness, even in many of the population centers in Best-Places books that come out on top statistically. Blandness has enveloped these places; architects, zoning experts, planners, corporations and automobile determinism have led to urban, suburban and small-town layouts that don't consider the needs of things like human beings.

Simplistic planners have not been able to distinguish between congestion and density. Congestion is too many people trying to get somewhere through too few paths. Density is people living in proximity with people. The first is alienating but the second can be humanizing. With a sweeping stroke, planners attacked congestion and brought down density with it, thereby separating people from each other.

Since congestion was primarily a product of the automobile, and since few people doubted the automobile's future status as supreme icon, much of the planning centered around facilitating the flow of automobiles.

In *The Geography of Nowhere*, James Howard Kunstler describes how the American penchant for automobiles over the last half-century has degraded our surroundings and impoverished our culture: "We've turned American towns and cities into auto storage depots that only incidentally contain other things," he writes. "By subordinating so many aspects of our lives to the car, we have created places unworthy of affection."

In *The Great Good Place*, Ray Oldenburg laments the disappearing "third place" in our lives, after home and work, the informal gathering spot, a focal point in a community where folks would just hang out. The physical characteristics of suburbia, the predominance of chain businesses, and the ideological dominance of work and profession are among the many contributors to America's greatest endangered species, the café or the friendly tavern. Television programs such as "Cheers" and its clones have become popular because they awaken our nostalgia for this disappearing phenomenon.

"Work, spend, work, spend" consumerism means that "some of the country's most popular activities have been turned into shopping expeditions," according to Juliet Schor, author of *The Overworked American: The Unexpected Decline of Leisure*. The author adds:

"We spend three to four times as many hours a year shopping as our counterparts in Western Europe...Most homes are virtual retail outlets, with cable shopping channels, mail-order catalogs, toll-free numbers and computer hookups." Less leisure time means less hanging out with neighbors. More home shopping conveniences mean less human interaction as part of the economy.

In researching the allegations of these social critics, I found a reference book called *The Lifestyle Market Analyst*, which lists the top 10 lifestyles of cities across the nation. Sure, it can get cold in Buffalo, but it is hard to believe that "shopping by catalog" is the second most-frequent lifestyle of that great city, as it allegedly is in Laredo, Texas.

These modern sociological trends engender places that are alive statistically but dead aesthetically.

According to Kunstler, extreme separation and dispersion of what used to be compact towns and neighborhoods, where everything was within a ten-minute walk, "has left us with a public realm that is composed mainly of roads. And the only way to be in that public realm is to be in a car, often alone. The present arrangement has certainly done away with sacred places, places of casual public assembly, and places of repose. Otherwise, there remain only shopping plazas, the supermarkets and the malls. Now, American supermarkets are not designed to function like Parisian cafés. There is no seating, no table service...yet some shoppers will spend as much time as their dignity affords haunting the supermarket aisles because it is practically the only place where they can be in the public realm and engage in some purposeful activity around other human beings. Here they even stand the chance of running into someone they know. A suburbanite could stand on her front lawn for three hours on a weekday afternoon and never have a chance for a conversation."

Critical of the malling of cities, Roberta Brandes Gratz, in *The Living City*, argues that street life is the essence of an urban place. Good streets have evolved over time rather than resulting from some lofty plan. "Contrast, variety, detail, surprise, drama, nooks, compactness, mixture of functions, nothing static, nothing boring—these are some of the things that make up a lively, well-functioning street."

A mall, no matter what its location or how many cafés it has, is conceptually a point in space, discontinuous from all else. "People drive to it, park, use it, get back in their cars, and drive away. Since people are never just passing through, malls remain detached from all else around them.

"The first thing a suburban mall does when superimposed on an urban downtown is eliminate the street," Brandes Gratz writes. "Studies have shown a direct link between economic losses in downtowns and continued growth of shopping malls."

People like Roberta Brandes Gratz and James Howard Kunstler are part of a simmering reaction against a monolithic monocultural invader. This "New Urbanism" has sought to create dynamic communities, while a parallel reaction in other places, both urban and rural, has fought off the onslaught of suburban sprawl in varying ways, some planned, others largely spontaneous. Cafés are springing up where one can now feel the street as an extension of the home. Even Los Angeles, California, is finally completing metro lines to counteract the monopoly of the automobile, and planning to bring back residents of varying economic levels to its downtown. One need only recall, following the earthquake, the images of the buckled Santa Monica Freeway and the resulting daily traffic jams on lateral roads to realize just how dependent we have become on one single mode of transportation.

The automobile and the shopping mall are but two of many alienating modern institutions that destroy the sense of place. Home entertainment, including cable TV, keeps people in their cocoons. Single-use zoning has made for bland neighborhoods where the corner store is no longer within walking distance. Back decks keep folks out of the sight of their neighbors. (To offset this last dehumanizing feature, the California city of San Luis Obispo recently passed an ordinance to encourage front porches on new homes.)

Corporate uniformity squeezes out alternative livelihoods. Handmade crafts, scavenging and street vending, to name a few niches for non-conformists or misfits, are endangered means of subsistence. Ma-and-pa stores, direct marketing of produce and other traditional businesses for the "little guy" have been livelihoods under siege. Show me a neighborhood with no ma-and-pa groceries and no street economy, and I'll show you a dull place with barren, sterile streets.

In his *Streets For People*, the confirmed peripatetic Bernard Rudofsky wrote: "It simply never occurs to us to make streets into oases rather than deserts." He wrote this "primer for Americans" in order illustrate countries where the function of streets has "not yet deteriorated into highways and parking lots."

No wonder so many Americans vacation in places where they can simply walk the animated streets and savor the vivid colors and rough-hewn textures, the collage of sounds, the contradictory aromas. These excursions are escapes from the daily dose of sensory deprivation.

I once did a survey of foreign students, asking them to descibe their first impression of the United States. There was a wide variety of responses, but by far the leading answer was: "there are no people in the streets."

FunkyTowns USA has done the research and found which locations have turned back the wave of uniformity and monoculturalism. Which cities, towns or neighborhoods have not succumbed to bland single-use zoning? Which ones remain independent of the politics that has led to the homogenizing of the USA? Which places staunchly maintain unconventional regional customs that make them fun to be in? Which ones are eccentric in their cultural tradition, and which ones remain unique thanks to the influence of bizarre geopgraphy? Which places defy the global, corporate economy and welcome alternative livelihoods? Which places display a level of tolerance that protects their non-conformists and makes one proud to be different?

Since the massive growth of suburbs in the fifties, this country has taken a straight and flattened path, as symbolized by the dull Interstate highway system. *Funky* is a metaphor for alternatives to the straight path.

In this book, we will try not to fall into the trap of elite judgmentalism. While *Places Rated* uses statistics on symphony orchestras and opera and dance companies in order to rate the level of culture, we think all musics are created equal and that blues, jazz, bluegrass and the likes deserve to be rated. Neither jazz nor bluegrass are any more part of the mainstream white-bread consumer music than opera or chamber music.

In the arena of education, we agree with *Places Rated* that dollars spent on education and pupil-teacher ratios are indeed vital statistics. We agree with *The 100 Best Towns in America* that public education expenditure is important.

However, what about the willingness of a school system to undertake radical experimentation, in order to save children from one-dimensional thinking, and what about a place's setting and ambience as it contributes to growing up? As a proponent of funkyism, I don't want my kids in a school that produces perfect automatons. The educational philosophy of a school system is at least as important as its expenditure per pupil.

Recently, while revisiting Los Angeles, California, I stopped with my wife to eat in a Mexican restaurant on Lankershim Boulevard, the old downtown of North Hollywood. When the proprietor of the restaurant went to the bandstand and sang along with a recording of a soulful tune, the mainstream part of me reacted as if the guy could have used some medical attention in the uppermost part of his body.

He then stepped forward and invited the diners to come up and perform. A lady from the back of the room, one who looked like a street person from nearby Magnolia Boulevard, was the next to take to the stage. In spite of her questionable talents, she received a round of applause. It was a rare occasion when people in a restaurant were suddenly dining together rather than alone at separate tables.

The proprietor asked me if I wanted to "perform". I was on the verge of saying yes. While I lacked the courage to get up there and display a healthy bit of exhibitionism, I did make a request. Were there any Jacques Brel songs available?

The proprietor found one, put the tape on, and "performed" my request. Later, other patrons stepped forward to sing along. Some might say this was a tacky event! But it brought people together and created an atmosphere where, for a brief moment in an age when people are increasingly alienated from each other, human beings were encouraged to reverse the process of estrangement. Do the same thing in another less friendly setting and we might be carted off to the nearest cuckoo's nest.

We believe that the physical and attitudinal setting conducive to bringing people out of their fortresses is a powerful point-getter when rating places.

One result of modern zoning laws is what Kunstler calls, "the monotony and soullessness of single-use zoning, which banished the variety that was the essence of our best communities." What has happened, essentially, is the elimination of the public realm and the exaltation of privacy. Whole regions have strived to minimize the possibility of contact between people and especially people of different cultures or economic backgrounds.

I was living in France during the construction of EuroDisneyland. Had the Disney management consulted with my neighbors, they would have learned ahead of time why such a place was not going to attract the projected number of tourists. Disneylands thrive in the U.S. in part because they offer a rendition of the traditional main street, something that we long for since such streets have been zoned out or depressed economically by shopping centers on the outskirts of town. In France, city centers in both cities and towns continue to thrive. There is no nostalgia or sense of loss that prompts the need for a make-believe downtown, such as the ill-conceived "City Walk," in Universal Studios, near Los Angeles, where one must arrive by car into an immense parking structure: in other words, another glorified mall.

Disney offers castles. In France they have preserved their own *chateaux*. What would you prefer, a make-believe castle, or the real living historical site? Disney offers experiences with lifestyles of the past that have disappeared as a result of a modern corporate economy. Although France has situated itself in the modern economy, it has preserved older lifestyles, such as the family farmer, the cheese maker and the wine maker. Thus, the French family wishing to gain contact with the past may do so directly. No theme park is necessary.

Many of the things fantasized in Disneyland are still around in France and other parts of Europe. Instead of the people mover in Tomorrowland, or the one in Detroit that passes through a wasteland of sensorially dead streets and unfriendly buildings, France has the "train a grande vitesse" (TGV), the real thing, with a social purpose.

Whole sections of Disneyland attempt to create a sense of place, which we look for nostalgically since our own sense of place has been devastated.

One of the unplanned causes of the European survival of "place" has been the exorbitant price of gasoline. The result is a public transportation system that is efficient and allows people of all backgrounds to mingle. Street musicians play in metro trains and corridors. Homeless people hang out there on benches. Professionals go to work in the metro. In fact, even some managers at the auto company, Renault, where I was teaching English, used public transportation to get to work.

With a serious network of public transportation, there comes a preservation of public places, street life and communities. In fact, the street, the café, the local park are considered extensions of one's home, and for this reason, the French do not view the amount of space in their home as a major requirement for a positive lifestyle. There is a balance between public and private space.

Many places in the United States have become entirely private space. One would think that being private allows one to maintain individuality. But when I have taken friends and relatives out of their suburban neighborhoods into my funky places, they relish the casual contact with unusual people.

I want the right to be unusual myself. Even the insane should have this right, as they do in traditional Latin American towns, where they are adopted and protected by the community, instead of being concealed from the neighbors.

This book is a celebration of those places in the United States of America that have maintained their uniqueness and diversity, while fighting off the incursions of the corporate monoculture. There is no common denominator that determines which places qualify. Thus, there will be great variation from one funky place to another. There is no attempt here to replace one monoculture with another.

The human geography of this book represents a rebellion against the "geographical correctness" of urban planners, modernist architects and zoning zealots. The diverse set of standards used here to evaluate places assures that we will not simply substitute one new monolithic dimension for the old one.

Finally, a place's acceptance of "different" ways of life and behaviors includes a tolerance of victimless fringe activities in

14

the realm of sex and gambling that our fundamentalist Calvinist heritage would condemn, as well as a social atmosphere where people who have made serious mistakes with their lives are given a second chance.

The standards used to derive the ratings in *FunkyTowns USA* blend objective measures with intuitive analysis. I hope that this rating method will evaluate sense of place in a much deeper manner than would a purely statistical approach. For some places, grading categories may overlap; if this happens, the points will be adjusted accordingly.

As far as the research is concerned, I have relied to a certain degree on my own living and traveling experience, having resided in New York, Chicago, Los Angeles and the Washington, D.C. area, and having traveled in 47 of the 50 states.

However, in order to provide balance, I have done extensive research, referring to both primary and secondary sources, using libraries across the nation, including the Library of Congress. Rather than disrupt the text with footnotes, all written sources of information are listed in a bibliography at the end of the book.

Finally, I have hunted down residents from the places considered for this book, using interviews with the most perceptive and critical of these residents as a primary component of our analysis. Even with places I felt I know most intimately, I sought out other opinions.

The interview portion of my research has been the most pleasing. Sometimes, lacking word-of-mouth connections, I would come across the name of a person quoted in an article, and if the quote seemed to voice an affinity for what this book was seeking, I would call directory assistance, most of the time coming up with the right phone number.

I must thank the people who provided me with details and analysis, so many of whom may have been unnerved by a phone call from a strange guy looking for peculiar information.

Having traveled over these unconventional roads for discovering the USA, I can safely conclude that whatever power structure is in place will never exercise total economic or cultural hegemony. There will always be alternative places for iconoclasts, misfits, cultural rebels, utopians, retrohippies, diehard traditionalists and radical activists.

Finally, a painstaking effort has been made to be current with all information in the book. Two days before handing in the final draft, I went down to Adams-Morgan to eat at the Picasso Café. I had recommended its eclectic food. But the Picasso Café had disappeared.

My research has been as up to date as is humanly possible and I apologize in advance if one or two establishments mentioned in the book have moved or gone out of business. One restaurant's skipping town is not going to alter the sense of place as we portray it here.

SUMMARY OF EVALUATION SYSTEM

 ore points are given for the broadest categories. Places may earn part credit within any category.

Unconventional Regional Customs (6 points)
Peculiar local identity that distinguishes one place from others.

Bizarre Geographic or Climatic Variations (6 points)
Where there are greater changes in terrain and climate within a smaller area, residents/visitors have more options/dimensions of living.

Cross-Cultural (5 points)
Where different kinds of people interact in a genuine way, meaning that one's physical or lifestyle differences will be most tolerated and appreciated.

Public Hangouts (5 points)
Profusion of "3rd places"(beyond work and home), for hanging out. Could be cafés, laundromats, highly frequented park bench areas, public squares, etc.

Non-Mainstream Recreation/Entertainment (5 points)
Standard tourist spots need not apply here.

Pedestrian Friendly (4 points)
Goods and services within walking distance. Layout and setting conducive to the pace and sensorial pleasures of pedestrian culture. Convenient public transportation to alleviate car dependency.

Mixed-Use Zoning & Layout (4 points)
Where different activities (commerce, recreation, housing) are not segregated into bland, single-function neighborhoods.

Upended Facilities (3 points)

Normal functions reconsidered. Old factories converted to housing, theaters in warehouses, etc.

Independent Politics (3 points)

Where neither Democrats nor Republicans have significant power. Where independent candidates have won elections. Where alternative decision-making thrives.

Alternative Economy (3 points)

Farmers markets, subsistence peddlers, street entertainers, channels for the sale of locally produced work.

Legal Positive-Expectation Gambling (2 points)

Not about frauds like lotteries and slot machines, but rather, games of skill where the studious player has a chance to win (horse racing, sports betting, poker and blackjack).

Freedom in the Bedroom (2 points)

Where sexual intolerance is not part of the dominant culture. With no access to strangers' bedrooms and without funds to hire voyeurs, we cheated in this category by using, as a yardstick, statistics on legislation prohibiting discrimination on the basis of sexual orientation. The existence of such laws, even when referring primarily to gays and lesbians, indicates a tolerance for any victimless sexual behavior, regardless of sexual persuasion.

Twelve categories in all, plus 2 "free points" for traits not fitting within the above parameters. Highest possible total is 50 points.

Welcome to FunkyTowns USA

ADAMS-MORGAN, WASHINGTON, D.C.

During the period of the 1954 Brown vs. Board of Education ruling, Morgan School was black and Adams School was white. The two principals got together in 1955 because they wanted to make a better neighborhood. From their union, the name Adams-Morgan stuck with this community.

Since then, Adams-Morgan has become one of the most vibrant multicultural communities in the USA. While nearby Georgetown loses several layers of diversity because of gentrification, Adams-Morgan remains accessible to a more eclectic mix of social, ethnic and economic backgrounds.

"On alternatively quiet and raucus streets," writes Barbara Raskin, "haves and have-nots live next door to each other, constantly surprised by their coexistence."

One of the have-nots is a guy who hangs out on 18th Street.

"What a beautiful dress you got on," he says to my daughter, as we stroll by. "Just wanted to let you know. I'm the Compliment Man."

Like many of our eccentric places, Adams-Morgan has active citizens' organizations that remain on guard against sieges from the corporate and governmental powers that would like to straighten it out.

Pedestrian Friendly (4 pts)

One of these recent incursions comes from D.C.'s previous mayor, who catalyzed a plan for a six-tier parking garage. Adams-Morgan representative, Steve Coleman, responded:

"Cars do not encourage people. Cars encourage the idea that you can't be on the sidewalk. We want to bring lots more people to Adams-Morgan," he added, promoting a frequent shuttle bus from the nearest metro station.

Mayor Kelly's garage would be "like dumping a Tyson's Corner (typical suburb) parking structure into a neighborhood that's known for its pedestrian nature."

Sure, parking is virtually impossible on weekend nights, unless one leaves the car in a nearby neighborhood and walks a half mile. But once a fast shuttle bus linking Adams-Morgan with the nearest metro stop is ready to roll, fewer cars will congest the streets.

Meanwhile, with the community battling against the garage, the city will have to change the zoning ordinance to get to first base on the project.

Various pedestrian-friendly features include numerous wall murals, kinky architecture and storefronts, and a lively and varied street population, including an occasional panhandler. Most notable are the weird windows on many buildings. If you can find a window with no sculpted frame or without peculiar arches, the elaborate cornices above will save the building from normality.

Free walking tours by travel expert Tony Pitch allow visitors to learn about the people behind the brick facades. Show up at 11:00 A.M. on Sunday, weather permitting, outside the Wyoming Apartment Building, 2022 Columbia Road.

One of the best walks in D.C. begins in Adams-Morgan. Take Columbia Road southwest until it runs into Connecticut Avenue. In less than a mile, you'll be in Adams-Morgan's companion in funk, Dupont Circle. The Dupont Circle neighborhood is a notch or two more upscale than Adams-Morgan but around every corner lurks a pleasant surprise.

Public Hangouts (5 pts)

I just happened to be in Adams-Morgan during the World Cup of Soccer. The restaurants and bars draped banners announcing that they were showing the games of this international sports event. It occurred to me that in Adams-Morgan I could choose my World Cup venue according to the team that was playing. I could see Nigeria in one of several African restaurants, Mexico in Mexican restaurants or at a hole-in-the-wall beer hall that reminded me of East L.A., Ireland in an Irish Pub, Morocco in a Couscous place surrounded by bookshelves with weathered classics from around the world.

Most of these spots are not of the in-and-out variety. In fact, the slow service in some of them is a subtle way to tell us that we need not be in any rush.

Alternative Economy (2 of 3 pts)

There's a major difference between the street vendors in Adams-Morgan and those that hang out by the Smithsonian museums on the D.C. Mall. All you can find on the mall are tacky tee-shirts or sweatshirts with words like "Washington" printed on them, along with the same old slice of pizza and hot dog. Meanwhile, in Adams-Morgan, here and there are crafts from various countries that represent the local population, with a raunchy flea market up and down Columbia Road. The other difference between The Mall and Adams-Morgan is price. You expect to get a good deal from a street vendor and in Adams-Morgan you do.

At night time there are free-lance parking attendants who jump into a scarce vacated space and motion to you that it's free, in exchange for a finder's fee.

Mixed-Use Zoning (4 pts)

With the exception of a few limited addresses, commerce is only allowed at street level, which means that the upper floors of the 14th Street and Columbia corridors are left for residents. Most of the exceptions are on 14th Street, where there is dancing on several second floors of restaurants, and rooftop dining at two others. The exceptions serve to highlight the rule; this is still a mixed-use community.

Cross-Cultural (5 pts)

The cultures, too, are mixed. African Americans, Central Americans and Angloamericans mingle with numerous other national groups. Adams-Morgan is the back yard of Embassy Row. In particular, there's a strong African presence, most notably from Ethiopia and Eritria. That continent is represented by various restaurants. The Bukom Café, named for a square in Ghana, serves dishes from Nigeria, Ghana, Ivory Coast, Senegal, Benin, Sierra Leone and Togo, along with jazz with an ethnic flavor. The place comes alive after 11:00 P.M. Just as a Mexican restaurant is not "foreign" in East L.A., Ethiopian restaurants in Adams-Morgan are part of the fabric of the community.

Some places are so cross-cultural that you can't label the food by country of origin. On one occasion I was able to uncover an explanation for the eclectic food; the cook was from New Orleans, where all cultures converge.

Adams-Morgan community groups have multicultural participation and the place itself acts as a bridge, as it straddles Rock Creek. West of Rock Creek is the white part of D.C., while to the east is the black section. If any one neighborhood can bring the city together it is Adams-Morgan.

Non-Mainstream Recreation/Entertainment (3 of 5 pts)

According to Tony Pitch, the best views in all of D.C. are from the apartment rooftops of Adams-Morgan. The only problem is, how do you get there to look down on the Capitol, the Smithsonian, the Potomac River and RFK Stadium?

Here are a few ideas. Most of the buildings have apartment managers. (1) Ring the manager's bell and tell him you are a member of The Drifters singing group and you are looking for a rooftop to film a music video of "Up On The Roof." (2) Find a building with a For Sale sign and tell the manager you are interested in buying. (3) Tell the manager you are a reporter with The Inquirer and need a perch to look down on Bill and Hillary's window in the White House. (4) Tell a local minister that you are a descendant of the hunchback of Notre Dame and wish to climb up the church spire.

When you get back down to the street, stroll over to Café Lautrec, on 18th Street. The music begins at about 10:00 P.M., a jazz trio. After a few songs, the tap dancer arrives and you wonder where he's going to dance, since there's hardly room for the musicians. He vaults atop the wide hardwood bar and the place begins to swing. Unlike other club performers, this guy wants your strict attention, and he lets you know. With his tapping as a fourth instrument, the swinging trio has become a funky quartet. The food is mainly French and the prices are reasonable, with no cover charge.

There are numerous other music and dance clubs along 18th Street, and a few on Columbia, some that have Sunday afternoon entertainment. Outside of Africa itself, only Paris offers more in the way of African music and dance.

Finally, one of the nation's funkiest festivals is Adams-Morgan Day, held in September. Most festivals give themselves a fancy name. Such a promotional device is not necessary for this street scene. The name Adams-Morgan itself broadcasts to people from Maryland to Virginia that it's okay to be weird. A companion annual festival, more traditional but no less entertaining, is International Day, celebrated in late August.

When the new shuttle is ready, D.C.'s free Smithsonian zoo, with its surviving panda, will be a skip away. Walking buffs will find both the zoo to the northwest and the various free Smithsonian museums, straight south, within reach.

Unconventional Regional Customs (2 of 6 pts)

Washington, D.C. remains a city of largely segregated neighborhoods. Adams-Morgan is integrated. Often, integrated neighborhoods have powerful institutions that keep white people in the neighborhood: for example, the University of Chicago in Hyde Park. Adams-Morgan's integration is grass roots, bottom up. Whereas Hyde Park is a middle class neighborhood, Adams-Morgan integrates all classes.

Other neighborhoods that seek to preserve various architectural periods accept gentrification as the lesser of evils when confronted with "development," but Adams-Morgan remains unmanicured, rough-edged and down to earth.

In its struggle against the automobile and in favor of the pedestrian, Adams-Morgan is a consummate iconoclast.

There are also institutions within the community that provide visionary support for the mentally ill and the homeless. "People with mental illness who come through our door," says Michael Benjamin, of The Green Door, "often find themselves leaving as taxpaying citizens."

Bizarre Geography (1 of 6 pts)

Adams-Morgan borders on Rock Creek Park, a deep, green gash that splits Washington, D.C. in two from north to south. Once down in the creek, it's a completely different world. H.G. Wells could have used this spot as a basis for The Time Machine II. The best way to get there from Adams-Morgan is by bicycle. On the north side of Columbia Road, just east of 18th Street, there's a large bicycle rental shop.

Freedom in the Bedroom (2 pts)
The District of Columbia has a comprehensive set of statutes that ban discrimination based on sexual orientation.

Positive-Expectation Gambling (1 of 2 pts)
Laurel Race Course to the north and Rosecroft Raceway to the south offer extensive menus of pari-mutuel horse wagering, both live and simulcast, days and nights. Adams-Morgan loses a point in this category because of the commute to these places. The lack of freeways out of D.C. makes the trip longer, but helps the community maintain its character. The trade-off is worth it.

Adams-Morgan's monumental struggle to be itself involves a long series of apparently trivial fights with the bureaucracy. For example, the District government is trying to force food-related commercial establishments to have indoor trash rooms. While "certainly desirable for trash control," said one community advocate, such a requirement would be "too expensive and restrictive for many of the small, cramped, low-profit carry-outs and grocery stores in our neighborhood."

It would only take a few of these apparently innocuous government regulations drawn up by well-meaning but myopic bureaucrats to transform a thriving neighborhood into a bland wasteland. Adams-Morgan will have none of this. So what if the alley stinks from time to time!

TOTAL POINTS: 29

APPLEGATE VALLEY, OREGON

Applegate Valley is situated off tiny Route 238, between Grants Pass and Medford, Oregon. With Interstate 5 bypassing Applegate, many travelers have no idea that a small detour would take them to a place "where the clock stopped in 1971," with the best, and maybe the only tree-house resort in the nation.

Gary Quester, a county resident, calls the Applegate Valley a place of "retrosixties people who went to Woodstock I but didn't go to Woodstock II."

Unconventional Regional Customs (4 of 6 pts)

The hippie label is too limited; the area is also populated by urban refugees and unemployed loggers, with horseback as the preferred medium of transportation. A back-to-nature philosophy is epitomized by Michael Garnier's Up N About, a "resort" where visitors stay in tree houses.

Alternative Economy (3 pts plus 2 bonus pts)

Various odd customs of the area relate to its alternative economy. Up N About has been hassled by the regional authorities because it doesn't come near what "normal" people conceive as a resort. First, the "housing" bureaucrats said the tree houses were not safe. So Garnier gave a 4th of July party and invited 66 friends up into his main tree house, along with the Weighmaster from Medford.

The 66 people along with two dogs ended up weighing 10,822 pounds. The tree house had passed the stress test. But the planning commission didn't give up, attempting to nail him on a zoning regulation. For some time, the resort has continued to operate by way of a loophole. Visitors don't pay for their "room." Instead, they buy an Up N About "tree-shirt," and having done so, they are invited to stay in the tree house at no charge.

This system may be altered with a November, 1994 ruling by county commissioners, previously referred to by "tree musketeers" as the "tree stooges." Under the new ruling, tree houses, properly constructed, can get a building permit.

When it comes to alternative economy, Garnier's business is just the tip of the iceberg, or rather, the edge of the forest. Many residents around the unincorporated village of Takilma pick exotic mushrooms and sell them to Japan. Herb pickers find plants that are needed in Mexico, Japan and China, or purchased by herbalists in the U.S. "Think global, act local," is much more than a slogan to Applegate Valley residents.

Modern anthropologists take note; you don't have to travel to remote areas of rural Africa or a secluded rainforest to find a culture of gatherers.

Other residents engage in arts and crafts and sell their wares on the fair circuit, or to various importers who show up in the region.

The nearby town of Ruch holds a big barter fair the first weekend in October; with this primitive economy, valley residents can maintain an independent standard of living without becoming part of the consumer society.

Independent Politics (3 pts)

Many folks who are disenchanted with our two dominant parties look to third-party candidates who, in essence, are taking some ideas from Republicans and others from Democrats without straying beyond the limits of those ideologies.

In Applegate Valley, independent politics means living truly beyond the boundaries of the current political system.

Non-Mainstream Recreation (1 of 5 pts)

While white river rafting is common to many regions of the USA, the local version is considered among the toughest challenges for rafters, since the Illinois River, a tributary of the Rogue River, is literally off the mainstream and can be quite treacherous.

For some alternative ways of life, theory is easier than practice; there is a necessary degree of compromise with the mainstream. In this pastoral region of Oregon, at the edge of national forests, just north of the California border, practice and theory are one.

TOTAL POINTS: 13

ARCATA, CALIFORNIA

olks have nicknamed the northern California city of Arcata "Sixties by the Sea," but the weirdness of this town cannot be pigeonholed in any way. The All-Species Parade, the Kinetic Sculpture Race and the public park at the Waste Water Treatment Plant, renamed "the Bird Sanctuary," are but a few peculiar images of this small city.

Bizarre Geography (4 of 6 pts)

Two miles from benign Pacific Ocean currents, the winter temperature rarely dips below 40 degrees, while the summer keeps comfortable in the 60s and 70s. Yet, six miles inland, at Blue Lake, summer temperatures will be 15 degrees hotter, while it will get much colder in the winter. Less than 30 minutes from town is Willow Creek, where hot-weather lovers can have their 90 degrees plus.

Arcata is situated between three nationally known natural attractions: Redwood National Park, Six Rivers National Forest and Avenue of the Giants. Old growth redwood trees on one side, the rugged Pacific coastline on the other. Even within the city limits, there is a majestic Redwood Park.

One can camp on a beach one day and in the forest and mountains the next.

Unconventional Regional Customs (6 pts)

What would have happened if the sixties culture had matured instead of disappearing or being co-opted? Perhaps the best place to find out is Arcata. Companies detrimental to the environment are kept out while human beings express their solidarity with the local ecology by marching in the All Species Parade, where participants must design a costume representing a regional animal, mineral or plant.

Numerous activist groups hold out in this city that voted itself a nuclear free zone, and whose City Council made a symbolic vote in favor of amnesty for those who did not want to serve in the Gulf War. If sixties folk seemed strange back in the sixties, those who have persisted into the nineties, whether you like them or not, deserve an award for perseverance against the tide of history.

Shopping mall culture is foreign to Arcata. In fact, many of its shops feature locally made handcrafted items.

Poster art publicity in the tradition of Toulouse-Lautrec has not been eclipsed by electronic advertising.

Cross-Cultural (1 of 5 pts)

Although Arcata does not have a very diverse population, the presence of Humboldt State College and the international activism of many local residents assure a modicum of crosscultural opportunities.

The Redwood Coast Dixieland Festival (March), Bebop and Brew (May), Jazz On The Lake (June) and Reggae On The River (August) are area music festivals that display a taste for this variety.

Public Hangouts (3 of 5 pts)

You can't miss The Plaza. Residents of all persuasions find this the place to be. Hangouts can't be planned, they just seem to happen, and no one can explain just why Los Bagels has become another popular community gathering place.

Some merchants have complained about Food For People serving the homeless in The Plaza during prime shopping hours. The program continues, in conflict with a judge's order that it does not meet sanitary requirements.

"It's not a serious problem," said one woman. "I'm an older person and I go to The Plaza all the time. I find no animosity from the homeless and there's a police officer patrolling on a bicycle."

The most bizarre hangout is called "The Bird Sanctuary," whose incongruous location is Arcata's world renowned Waste Water Treatment Plant, truly a town gathering place.

Upended Facilities (3 pts)

The way people gather at cafés in some towns, they hang out at The Waste Water Treatment Plant in Arcata. Encompassing 75 acres of former landfill, it now has a series of marshes that naturally treat Arcada's wastewater before it is released into Humboldt Bay. Bird watching, jogging trails and views of the bay and foothills abound.

Downtown there is the store, Jacoby's Storehouse, resuscitated from the 1850s when it served as an outlet for goldminers' materials.

The Minor Theatre, built in 1914, is comprised of three restored structures that today show current, classic and artistic films in an atmosphere of interior and exterior craftsmanship.

Throughout Arcata, walls of buildings become canvases for art work. The Arcata Chamber of Commerce supplies mural guide literature.

Alternative Economy (3 pts)

Twice a week, from May through November, the Arcata Plaza becomes a progressive open-air farmers market with a full range of fresh fruit, vegetables and flowers.

In and around the Plaza, you'll find a flower stand, an oriental rug seller, a Mexican food stand, and Humdoggers: if you don't like their hot dogs and polish sausages, you can order tofu.

Many of the products sold in shops have been crafted by local residents, while Arcata citizens' artwork is put on display in restaurants, businesses and government offices.

Pedestrian Friendly (4 pts)

Arcata is street-friendly in both its intimate size and the character of its surroundings. There are a number of attractive Victorian homes, wall murals, landmark buildings, The Plaza, art galleries, and artistic poster publicity reminiscent of the streets of Paris.

Independent Politics (3 pts)

Local political leaders are neither Democrats or Republicans. In fact, there are no political parties. People run for local seats without party affiliation, later passing all kinds of weird legislation, much of it symbolic of the town's identity.

Mixed-Use Zoning (4 pts)

Commerce and residence are not segregated from each other and downtown has not been depressed by regional malls. Arcata makes extensive efforts to preserve, revitalize and restore the architectural structures of the past, and has an active program to protect the city's structures and features.

Non-Mainstream Recreation (4 of 5 pts)

The North Country Fair, a mid-September equinox harvest event, is unlike any other fair in the world. "The Same Old People" who sponsor the fair, are not the same people every time, and the fair itself metamorphizes from year to year. What truly sets it apart from other fairs is its All Species Parade and the North Coast Environmental Ball, where the best species costumes receive awards.

Participants may dress as any animal, vegetable or mineral from the region. "The environmentalist consciousness is very strong," says one participant, Winchell Dillenbech, a refugee from New York who has lived in Arcata for more than twenty years.

What if the Indianapolis 500 were fused with an art fair? Well, the Arcata region offers an alternative to "the 500" on Memorial Day weekend with its Annual World Championship Great Arcata-to-Ferndale Cross-Country Kinetic Sculpture Race.

Kinetic Sculptures are human-powered works of art designed to travel over all terrain (roads, sand, mud and water). The race itself is a highly sophisticated work of art, quite "moving," you might say.

There are awards for design, music (some racing sculptures make music), performance and the special award for finishing dead middle of the pack. Two recent awards went to racing vehicles designed as an iguana and a banana.

Other unusual experiences are not limited to annual schedules. Fishing (Eel River), horseback riding, mountain biking or swimming are not in themselves out of the ordinary, but they become extraordinary when taking place *within an old-growth redwood forest*, nature's equivalent to the Gothic Church, amidst trees up to 1,500 years old and as tall as 350 feet.

Also, there are the dunes preserves at Mad River Beach County Park and numerous other zany regional festivals.

The redwood experience is "heightened" by the fact that the Arcata Community Forest, all 575 acres of it, is located within the city limits, and thus, within walking or bicycling distance.

Freedom in the Bedroom (2 pts)

California's comprehensive laws barring discrimination based on sexual orientation and Arcata's roots in the sixties suggest a sexually tolerant place.

Long-time resident Winchell Dillenbach speaks highly of many local eateries, recommending, in particular, Folie Douce, for its excellent French food with great atmosphere as well. He touts the full duck dinner for about $15. He also speaks highly of the more moderately priced food at the Mexican booth on The Plaza. Another local resident lauds the Italian food at Abruzzi, within a wooded atmosphere.

There's good espresso at Ramone's Bakery, and as you'd expect in a sixties time warp place, vegetarians are not left out; there are the Wildflower Café and Bakery and The Tofu Shop Delicatessen.

Arcata is 289 miles north of San Francisco and 95 miles south of the Oregon border. According to Arcata's geographers, it is 5,716 miles from Paris.

Meals in most restaurants are quite reasonably priced. The average rent for a 2-bedroom apartment is $500. The unemployment rate in Humboldt County is characteristcially above the State average. Motel prices are moderate.

TOTAL POINTS: 37

AUSTIN, TEXAS

From the freeway, Austin looks like any central Texas city, sprawled out on the obscenely vast, overwhelming plain. As a result, many folks who are making the oppressive drive across the interminable state find no temptation to stop and check out the city.

Too bad. Austin is the converse of a mirage. In the distance, you think it's the same old cement nothingness, a glitch on the desert, when in fact it is a true oasis. Writer Michael Hirschorn says, "Austin's weirdness makes it a much more yeasty place to view the world...an outpost against the homogenization of American life..."

Sure, one might attribute Austin's uniqueness to the university, which accounts for a tenth of its residents. Like many college towns, this city's ambience is enhanced by near-campus cafés and saloons.

Bizarre Geography (4 of 6 pts)

But it's much more than that. To the northwest of the city is Hill Country, a prime area for suburban developers. In any other city, Hill Country would have been completely overrun by the real estate powers that be.

But springing from the hills are brooks and streams that lead right down into the city, producing a number of deep eddies and old-fashioned spring-fed swimming holes. Not many cities in the world can boast of this benevolent visitation of the country smack dab in the city.

Many fun-loving people, who under ordinary circumstances would not have become politicized, have formed grass roots organizations to protect their swimming holes from the inevitable contamination that would result if the developers were left unbridled in the hills.

Independent Politics (1 of 3 pts)

Grass roots organizations such as SOS (Save Our Springs) have "sprung" up to oppose the developers, in particular to protect Barton Spring's natural water hole. The outcome: initiatives have been passed to limit development, to protect the hills. Phil, an Austin resident, says these hills are "comparable to the Ozarks but for their relative dryness."

If Austin's politics are engaging from the bottom up, adds Phil, from the top down it's not so quixotic, because of the so-called "Gentlemen's Agreement," which sets aside one token city council seat for an African American and one for an Hispanic.

Unconventional Regional Customs (3 of 6 pts)

Although there is no obvious custom that separates Austin from the rest of the world, residents and observers alike point out that here is a place where a "different" person can feel comfortable. Perhaps this explains the existence of Hippie Hollow, a clothing optional natural pool in a Lake Travis cove, to the northeast. "If you don't want to be offended by nude people," Police Sgt. Thomas Silakowski was quoted in *Newsweek*, "don't go to Hippie Hollow."

Many people who are not of the nudist philosophy nevertheless choose to strip down and go skinny-dipping in the old swimming hole.

On the bluff above Hippie Hollow is a funky restaurant called The Oasis, where folks gather to watch the sun go down. As the sun sets, one hears the applause. Perhaps an ex-Key West resident had something to do with initiating this long-standing Key West tradition in the heart of Texas.

Public Hangouts (5 pts)

The Oasis is just one of the many captivating Austin hangouts, in a city where, according to one observer, "It's as interesting a town to watch people in as any place I've seen." Our man Phil is proud that his town has lots of bar music, lots of clubs. He highlights Antone's, a popular blues club. And the swimming holes, too, function as public hangouts.

Pedestrian Friendly (2 of 4 pts)

As expected, in oil-producing Texas, the automobile is part of the ruling apparatus, but Austin does have its pockets where it feels good to be out on the street.

There are some street musicians on 6th Street, and "The Drag" (Guadalupe Street) has lots of life. Students from a local art course have produced some fine outdoor wall murals on old warehouses and at the base of parking structures, usually with Hispanic themes.

According to *Rough Guide USA*, "Austin is one of the few cities in the state where walking, cycling, and reading on the grass are more common than driving around in big cars."

Alternative Economy (1 of 3 pts)

While corporations still rule Texas, there are a few voids in the economy in Austin. There is a county-sponsored farmers market, every day in the north and on a vacant field in the south on weekends.

Other alternative economic niches: street vending on "The Drag" and microbreweries, thanks to a recent State law.

Mixed-Use Zoning (1 of 4 pts)

Redevelopment (as opposed to urban renewal) of older areas in town has encouraged some degree of mixed use.

Upended Facilities (1 of 3 pts)

Most notable is an old downtown warehouse which has been converted into theaters, restaurants and offices.

Non-Mainstream Recreation (1 of 5 pts)

Bat watching. The annual bat migration reaches its peak in August. A million and a half of these insect exterminators have their young and roost in Austin, especially under the Congress Avenue Bridge. At night they fly out in mile-long processions to banquet on 30,000 pounds of insects. One can watch them from a special observation area on the southwest corner of the bridge, or from a bat-watching cruise equipped with bat-shit protectors.

Freedom Of The Bedroom (2 pts)

Austin is the only city in Texas to pass a comprehensive set of civil rights laws that include the barring of discrimination based on sexual orientation.

Austin, moves us to add the optional 2 points. In Northern California, for example, it is easier to forge a different place than in Texas. Austin has to buck a lot of influences, the oppressive summers that keep people in air-conditioned cocoons, the build-now-ask-later ideology that has governed the growth of most Texas cities, the dependency on automobiles, fostered by the state's vast distances and powerful oil companies, and the fundamentalist tradition that has led the American Family Association's Mark Weaver to call the cops every time he sees a naked person by Hippie Hollow.

TOTAL POINTS: 23

BEREA, KENTUCKY

In an age of shopping malls and sophisticated global marketing, there's a certain defiance in producing something with your own hands and selling it directly to the consumer with no help from middlemen.

Alternative Economy (3 pts)

The town of Berea, Kentucky has managed to buck the trend of mass production and marketing, thanks to an innovative college with a mission. Berea College, which is virtually inseparable from the town itself, has used the regional craftmanship of Appalachia as focal point of its identity.

But if you expect courses in Underwater Basketweaving, think again. A large cadre of craftspeople reside in town: chair makers, potters, leathersmiths, stained glass experts, spoonmakers, weavers, quilters and more. Students who choose to study a craft must meet stiff requirements. If they excel, their products are sold around town, in places such as the Log House Sales Room on Jackson Street.

Unconventional Regional Customs (3 of 6 pts)

Crafts are but a portion of the college curriculum, which also specializes in liberal arts and agriculture. At a time when the cost of college tuition is skyrocketing on a par with health care, Berea College charges zero tuition, primarily serving low-income students from southern Appalachia.

In exchange for the free tuition, students work for ten or fifteen hours a week in any of 138 college-owned businesses.

Berea College did not become non-conformist overnight. It was founded in 1855 as the first interracial college in the South. It was then, as now, dedicated to educating those who otherwise might not be able to attend college.

To get an idea of its radical past, consider that four years after the college was founded, it was forcibly shut down by mobs opposed to its stand in support of abolitionist John Brown's raid at Harpers Ferry. In the pre-civil rights era, the State forced the college to become segregated. Today, although there are far fewer African American students, the college is known for its nurturing of all minorities.

Cross-Cultural (2 of 5 pts)

While the college serves the mainly white Appalachian population that characterizes its region, it strives for a cultural mix, with 5 percent of its students coming from out of the country. As a result of this policy, for example, Berea has the highest concentration of Tibetans in the U.S. One might say that the mountains of Appalachia meet the Himalayas, although to the Tibetans, the Appalachian Mountains appear as mere foothills.

Pedestrian Friendly (3 of 4 pts)

Berea has two town centers. Uptown is where you find the post office and city officials and downtown is College Square, where both traffic lights are always red, leaving pedestrians in total control. A city park and city-owned forest property with marked trails encourage extended walks.

Public Hangouts (2 of 5 pts)

Berea has two "coffee clubs." For a nominal fee, you gain the right to bring a coffee mug with your name on it and serve yourself at the Cardinal Deli or Berea Coffee and Tea. The "club" denotation means that regulars rather than in-and-outers create the atmosphere. The city park is another popular hangout.

Bizarre Geography (1 of 6 pts)

The setting for this cozy town is the area where Kentucky bluegrass country and Appalachia meet, a type of interior border between two fascinating cultures.

Positive-Expectation Gambling (2 pts)

Berea is located about thirty miles south of Lexington, the hub of horse race activities. When live racing is not in season, the simulcasting monitors keep you in action year round.

Back in town, locals recommend the southern dining at the Boone Tavern, staffed mainly by students from the college's Hotel Management program. The entrée comes with hot spoonbread, a moist cornmeal soufflé. This restaurant is featured in the venerable book, *Road Food*.

For healthy, low-cholesterol, mostly vegetarian food, there's The Peace Garden, also highly recommended by the townies.

Should you consider purchasing an item of craftswork, you will frequently have the chance of meeting the maker, and observing the manufacture at each stage of production. Recommended is Churchill Weavers, a landmark in town, the largest loomhouse in the U.S. where the original 1922 looms are still in use.

Although the town is the site of three major music festivals, you have to drive twelve miles south to Renfro Valley for bluegrass music.

TOTAL POINTS: 16

BURLINGTON, VERMONT

nly one Member of Congress in the entire United States is neither Democrat nor Republican. He is Bernard Sanders. The district that elected him includes the city of Burlington, Vermont. Before becoming a Member of Congress, Sanders served as Mayor of Burlington from 1981-89.

While most areas of the U.S. have representative democracy, the more participatory style of democracy has survived in Vermont, with Town Meeting Day as an annual state holiday. Among the legislation that has spun out of this grass roots scenario is Act 250, a tough set of environmental laws which, among other things, hold back the incursion of shopping malls. As a result, the ma-and-pa business districts of most Main Streets in Vermont have a greater survival rate than other comparable places; Vermont is the only state, for example, without a Wal-Mart.

Pressures from developers finally led to the construction of a couple of malls outside Burlington. But Article 250 and community activism gave the downtown area a head start and its dynamism seems to be irreversible.

Independent Politics (3 pts)

To have elected Bernie Sanders, an independent and avowed socialist, to Congress represents a major break from the Democrat/Republican plutocracy. According to James, a young man of Latin descent who resided in Burlington for four years, "Northern dairy areas with smaller operations seem to have a ruggedly independent electorate, places like Burlington and Madison, Wisconsin. They can elect conservatives, they can elect progressives, but they make that choice independently."

Cross-Cultural (1 of 5 pts)

James adds, critically, "If your skin color's different, you might not feel it so friendly, but Burlington is not a racist city." Since James left to take a job in Washington, grass roots activists have been working hard on the racial justice and equity issue, and Burlington's basic tolerance allows for this work to move forward. The Peace and Earth Store sells many craft items from the so-called Third World, purchased from collectives and wholesalers who are committed to non-exploitation and justice.

In early October, there is Marketfest, a celebration of Burlington's cultural diversity.

Pedestrian Friendly (4 pts)

Burlington's warm street atmosphere would not have survived had it not been for the town's active struggle to protect and preserve its downtown area. James says that he spent his four years without the need for a car. The rare times that something is not within walking distance, there is bus service which functions rather efficiently, at least during work hours.

Mixed-Use Zoning (4 pts)

One reason why you find people on the streets is that commerce and residence were not arbitrarily segregated in the name of city planning.

Upended Facilities (3 pts)

"Vacant waterfront warehouses were rehabilitated for shops, housing and restaurants," wrote Roberta Gratz. One example of an upended facility: Chassman & Bem, a major bookstore in Burlington which carries 80,000 titles, used to be an opera house.

Public Hangouts (5 pts)

If skiing is a major winter sport of the area, hanging out is an important spring-summer-autumn sport. Several blocks of Church Street have been closed off to motor traffic, but the extended downtown hangout of cafés and parks has not been artificially malled away from the rest of the city, since cross streets still pass through.

There are too many vibrant hangouts to enumerate here. One of the more eclectic and contrarian spots is the Last Elm Café, run by an anti-profit collective and featuring folk and other types of music. The menu is irregular. "You never know what you're going to get," says one resident. "One day it's gourmet and the next time it's mundane. You never know what musicians are going to show up. I saw 'Fish' play there." (If you haven't heard, Fish is a popular Vermont-based eclectic music group.)

Another non-profit spot is the multi-purposed shop mentioned above, the Peace and Earth Store, run by activists, and also housing a library of progressive newsletters.

Bookstores like Chassman & Bem sponsor readings by visiting authors. European-style outdoor cafés abound as do street benches. One regular explains her sensorial attachment to these outdoor hangouts: "Burlington sparkles."

Waterfront Park and the neo-Victorian Burlington Boathouse are places to enjoy the human and natural setting, including bicycle paths, lakeside parks and even beaches where one can swim.

To experience Central Park away from The Big Apple, 7 miles from downtown Burlington is the huge Shelburne Farms, whose parks and gardens were designed by Frederick Law Olmsted, the same landscape architect who conceived New York's Central Park. At certain points in this vast picnic area, one looks down on a splendid view of Lake Champlain.

Alternative Economy (1 of 3 pts)

While Burlington is too well-organized and bordering on chic, there is still room for alternative economies. We've mentioned a not-for-profit shop and restaurant. There is also a farmers market in which local crafts people must make their own products in order to be permitted to sell.

Bizarre Geography (1 of 6 pts)

The unusual north-south extension of Lake Champlain makes it necessary to provide some sort of transportation to the other side: New York's Adirondack region. But the lake's pristine beauty deters the most avid developers from building bridges. As a result, there are several spectacular ferry rides across the lake, equivalent to a poor man's cruise.

Unconventional Regional Customs (1 of 6 pts)

Although environmentalism in some ways is now part of the mainstream, the degree to which Burlington's public consciousness is rooted in the environment is extraordinary. For example, the continuing education 4-day workshops at Shelburne Farms concentrate specifically on environmentally-oriented agricultural concerns and ecological systems, and the city owes much of its preservation to the strength of Act 250.

Malls outside the city don't seem to be hurting the downtown, although some local business people say they feel the impact. Meanwhile, Burlington provides an off-beat point of departure for some of the best skiing and boating in the country.

Getting around this university town of 38,752 (1990 census) is quite easy. Visitors' maps and info on lodging and upcoming events are available at The Information Gallery, a kiosk on the corner of Church and Bank streets.

TOTAL POINTS: 23

CAJUN COUNTRY, LOUISIANA

Once one has the opportunity of communicating with people from Cajun Louisiana, it becomes apparent that what we call a "culture" defies all attempts at definition and categorization. Consider that the Cajuns originally descend from 10,000 Acadians (former 17th century French colonists), deported by the British from an area which now encompasses the cross-border of French Canada and the tip of Maine, centered around Madawaska.

About 5,000 Acadians remained at that time to preserve their way of life. While most of the deportees eventually ended up in south-central Louisiana, some landed as far away as the Falkland Islands. Today, when the folks from Madawaska reunite with their Cajun brothers and sisters, they find few things in common. For example, while the Acadians in Maine defend their culture in political ways, the Cajuns do so through music and cooking. Northern Acadian food is bland, hardly comparable with spicy Cajun food but for the one-pot cooking style.

Clearly, the radically different climates and economies, from northern Maine to southern Louisiana, have had much to do with the divergent customs of the two Acadian groups.

Cross-Cultural (2 of 5 pts)

The Cajuns are inherently cross-cultural. You can hear it in their mixture of English and French, with French words often wedged in for the more emotive connotations. Writer Bryan Miller refers to a land that "blends elements of the gritty rural south with those of ancestral maritime France."

Public Hangouts (5 pts)

Much has been written about Cajun dance halls, one of two types of public hangout that preserve a way of life. The other less publicized gathering place is the morning café, accompanied by a brand of coffee aptly named "Community." To the Cajuns this is strong coffee, but to others who did not grow up with it, it is "muddy."

"When we travel away from home," says Reggie, a former Mamou teacher, "we take a tin of our Community Coffee with us."

Although Cajun Country forms a large triangle pointing north, whose base nearly crosses the whole state at the bottom (excepting New Orleans), its heartland is no larger than greater Los Angeles. Moving counterclockwise and beginning at 12:00 on the compass, one can hop from gathering place to gathering place. This trajectory of spirited music and dancing covers the towns of Ville Platte, Mamou, Basile, Eunice and Breaux Bridge.

In Ville Platte, we are introduced to the local music at Floyd's Record Shop, which stocks recordings dating back to the 1930's.

After Floyd's you can put theory into practice by dancing at Snooks. In Mamou, there is Fred's Lounge, home of Don Thibodeaux's live Saturday morning radio program. Free samples of boudin, a Cajun sausage combining seasoned pork with rice, accompany beer, mixed drinks, and lots of two-stepping.

In tiny Basile, there is D.I.'s, offering music and food.

The next town is Eunice, home of the Liberty Center for the Performing Arts, a 1920s brick structure with a live evening radio show, Rendez-Vous des Cajuns. Also just outside of Eunice are Cajun jam sessions at the Savoy Music Center, a store run by music historians. Then there is Mulate's in Breaux Bridge, with live Cajun music seven nights a week, and all varieties of local cuisine, within an unusual building supported by beams from age-old, swamp cypress trees.

All of these towns have their local cafés. The morning conversation is just as lively as the music. The Cajuns I've interviewed are as agile and inventive in the art of conversation as they are with an accordion, perhaps in part because of their bilingual, colloquial heritage. We could name a few homespun cafés here, but Reggie says they're always changing their names.

Unconventional Regional Customs (3 of 6 pts)

The gathering does not stop with cafés and dance halls. Eating crawfish and drinking beer is a social occasion and not a mere dinner. Reggie adds that there are "suppers," where a group of men get together regularly to play cards while taking turns with the cooking. As a rule, Cajun men love to cook; Reggie gets a kick out of sharing recipes.

His students used to call him Mr. Reggie. They even call the principal by his first name.

"The town is like an extended family," he explains. "Joe just might be related to Mary and if you talk about Joe to Mary, you might be talking about somebody's cousin.

"Often, the big topic of conversation is who died. We make a gumbo right at the funeral home for the family of the deceased."

Non-Mainstream Recreation (3 of 5 pts)

Most of these towns have their own Mardi Gras celebrations, including elaborate ceremonies, wild street parties, free-for-all dancing, and lots of good eating. Annual festivals are nothing strange to most towns in the USA, but few can rival the Mardi Gras.

Meanwhile, weekly live radio programs, undented by the competition from TV, keep the party rolling year round.

On several occasions, while attending live presentations of Cajun music and dance, I have felt a greater parallel with the Mexican Norteña bar and street music than with anything French. Two-step dance styles, lively accordion melodies and bizarre lyrics are mainstays of both these scenes...

Quelle belle vie

Ma femme est partie

The partying continues in various local fetes, most notably the Breaux Bridge Crawfish Festival, a 3-day bash. Crawfish are miniature freshwater lobsters. They may be boiled or prepared "etoufée," smothered in sauce and stewed with scallions, onions and spices, served with the obligatory white rice.

At the Breaux Bridge festival, you use an insulated beer-can holder, worn around the neck, so that the arms are free for eating, dancing and expressing yourself.

Food festivals abound in surrounding towns. For example, Gonzales has its Jambalaya Festival (ham, chicken, sausage, fresh pork, shrimp and oysters, with shortening, onions, garlic and peppers, and of course, rice). Broussard has its Boudin Festival.

Bizarre Geography (1 of 6 pts)

The crawfish are crustaceans that live in the bayous, fresh water canals and marshes, where they burrow in mud. There is both deep-water and "pond" or farm-raised crawfish.

The western point of the Cajun triangle actually laps over the Texas line a few miles past Port Arthur and is referred to as "Cajun Lapland."

Cajun country is made up of four distinct geographical areas. The bayou country consists of fertile levee lands built up by natural process. Then, there are coastal marshes, rich with oil and gas, but today quickly eroding. The inland swamps in the Atchafalaya Basin are virtually uninhabited. Finally, there are the agricultural prairies, with mainly rice, cattle and soybeans. While Cajun has become "chic" nowadays, in the heartland of Acadiana, its smaller towns and their dance halls keep the "bons temps" rolling in the homespun way.

TOTAL POINTS: 14

CLARKSDALE, MISSISSIPPI

The blues is a genre of music and a state of mind. With it often seems to come a shedding of inhibitions and an unfettering of the soul. It was a product of plantation peonage. Branching out from this genre were both jazz and rock 'n' roll, two liberating forces that shook up the repressive fifties.

Most of us have had the opportunity to hear the blues in contemporary settings. But Clarksdale, Mississippi, in the heart of the Delta, offers us an experience with the blues in their original context.

Unconventional Regional Customs (4 of 6 pts)

At a time when customs evolve at a rapid pace or dissolve before the massive forces of uniformity and corporate capital, the blues culture of Clarksdale rolls on, uncontaminated, uncommercialized. This means that in spite of recent publicity, this home town of Robert Johnson (Eric Clapton's inspiration), Muddy Waters, W.C. Handy, B.B. King, John Lee Hooker, Bessie Smith, Sam Cooke and numerous other greats has maintained the honky-tonk, unmanicured and rough-edged setting of the blues.

Non-Mainstream Entertainment (and Public Hangouts) (6 pts)

Most of Clarksdale's juke joints are not pretty places. Two years ago, an *Economist* article suggested that the town should clean up its blighted Issaquena nightclub strip, where it is hit and miss as to what day and at what hour you'll hear the blues, and where places like the Blue Diamond Lounge continue to operate in boisterous and dimly lit locales.

"The tourists are coming," wrote Byron York in *The Washington Post*, "but—at least for now—not too many to spoil the place." While 90 miles north, Graceland receives 750,000 visitors annually, ironically Clarksdale, the site of the music that inspired Elvis Presley, only gets a small portion of that number. Presley's first record, "That's Alright Mama," was identified with Big Mama Thornton, a black blues singer.

Yet, with the city's resurgence, contemporary blues musicians such as Johnnie Billington are moving back to the area.

Among other local clubs are Smitty's Red Top Lounge, The Riverfront Lounge and Red's South End Disco, which, in typical fashion, has no sign and no address. It's just a building with a grey front and big blues.

Then there is the Delta Blues Museum (601/624-4461), housed in the public library and visited by people from all over the world, especially western Europeans. Without charge, the museum offers videotape and slide-and-sound programs, archives, performances, and memorabilia. Live blues concerts are scheduled once a month on museum grounds, which fits in with founder Sid Graves' mission of creating something "vibrant, alive—something the public can engage in."

"Some visitors from Europe have told me they came to the USA to see three things," said museum curator John Ruskey. "The Empire State Building, the Grand Canyon and the Mississippi Delta—home of the blues."

In and around town is an open-air museum of blues history, including Muddy Waters' home. At the local WROX radio station,

Early "the Soul Man" Wright has been broadcasting since 1947.

The town has more than its fair share of festivals, most noteworthy, the Sunflower River Blues Festival (early August), with local and national artists, and the Tennessee Williams Festival (mid-October). The famous playwright spent his childhood in Clarksdale.

Positive-Expectation Gambling (2 pts)

Along with the blues renaissance, also contributing to an expected economic recovery of the region is the renewal of an old tradition: riverboat gambling. Ten miles from Clarksdale is the Lady Luck Rhythm casino and only 35 miles down the road, over the county line, are the Casinos On The River.

Upended Facilities (1 of 3 pts)

Clarksdale's Riverside Hotel, with moderately priced room rates, was originally the Afro-American Hospital. Most people who go there ask to stay in Room No. 2, for $38 a night, since it was there, in that former operating room, that the dying Bessie Smith was brought after an auto accident in 1937. As a hotel, it is the former home of Sonny Boy Williamson, Ike Turner, the Staple Singers, the Five Blind Boys and many others.

W.C. Handy's home, on 317 Issaquena Avenue, is now a barber shop, which is a story in itself since it is operated by Wade Walton, the internationally renowned "Blues Barber."

Cross-Cultural (2 of 5 pts)

Clarksdale is a predominantly African American town with a black mayor. But a love for the blues has catalyzed interaction between blacks and whites on various levels. For many years, most of the people around town "just didn't know what they had," writes Byron York. "The whites knew the blacks were making music, but most of them didn't much care. The blacks knew it, and thought the rest of the world didn't care about Clarksdale, either."

This has all changed. The two main sectors of the city's population have now recognized that the blues heritage is for everyone to be proud of.

There is also a considerable Lebanese population. Resthaven Restaurant, formerly Chamoun's, serves authentic Lebanese cuisine.

Mixed-Use Zoning (2 of 4 pts)

Housing, commerce and entertainment are somewhat mixed together. Houses sell anywhere from $30,000 to $40,000, with a $60,000 maximum, while two-

and three-bedroom apartments rent for anywhere from $275 to $400.

The Alcazar Hotel, on the National Register of Historic Places, has an old-fashioned drug store and other small businesses on its first floor and is going to be restored into apartments for the elderly.

Pedestrian Friendly (2 of 4 pts)

In fact, Clarksdale's downtown is like an outdoor museum, with a T-junction on one end, looking upon some old forties buildings, and a railroad bridge on the other, providing focal points for the pedestrian. The Art Deco Greyhound station remains, as does a weather-beaten classic Coke advertisement, painted on the side of the red-brick building housing Jenkins Feed. Clarksdale's back-to-the-forties look is authentic and unadulterated.

For comprehensive information on Clarksdale, Mississippi, phone 800/626-3764.

TOTAL POINTS: 19

COLUMBUS, NEW MEXICO

ere is a town whose existence and livelihood are derived from the man who burned the place down in 1916: Pancho Villa. The helter-skelter layout of the town is virtually the same as it was at the time of Villa's attack.

Mixed-Use Zoning (4 pts)

Throw away the grids. Of all town layouts, Columbus's has to be the kinkiest. The modern Columbus cannot be molded into a ho-hum town. Asymmetrical Columbus earns the maximum rating for mixed-use zoning.

Bizarre Geography (2 of 6 pts)

Columbus is bypassed by Interstate 10, thirty miles to its north, and separated from El Paso, Texas by an uninhabited desert. Sergeant Gerard would have had a tough time finding Dr. Richard Kimble there. The weather is benign thanks to its plus- 4,000 feet altitude. History and geography allow this town to remain isolated from mainstream life. Had Kimble arrived here, he might have stayed at a Bed and Breakfast, "Helen's Hideaway."

Cross-Cultural (4 of 5 pts)

For a middle-of-nowhere place, one would expect a bland ambience, but Columbus is a border town. Its only newspaper is the bimonthly, English-Spanish *Las Fronteras*. Palomas, Mexico is nearer to its reality than Albuquerque or El Paso.

Pedestrian Friendly (2 of 4 pts)

Its small scale gives it an advantage in the within-walking-distance department. In fact, one could stash the car exclusively for vacations and weekend excursions. For those who make the pedestrian culture their primary code of existence, the three-mile walk to Palomas, Mexico would be an easy warm-up.

Upended Facilities (1 of 3 pts)

The local cultural center, The Tumbleweed Theatre, is now located at Martha's Place, a Bed and Breakfast. I've heard of dinner theater before, but bed-and-breakfast theater?

Unconventional Regional Customs (3 of 6 pts)

For health of body and wallet, pharmaceuticals can be found across the border for a fraction of the U.S. cost. Since Mexico's prescription laws are less stringent than ours, thinking adults who don't wish to pay a doctor for the prescription they know they need, may be able to legally make their purchase in Palomas.

The Columbus fire department and school system are made available to Palomas residents, thereby diminishing the effect of that unnatural line we call a border.

Columbus' most contrarian custom is its identity. Many of the town's features, including its State Park, are named for the man who raided the town in 1916. It was the second and last time that mainland USA has ever been invaded by a foreign power.

Naming places in Columbus after Villa seems tantamount to naming places in Pearl Harbor after Emperor Hirohito. But if my sources are correct, there was a certain legitimacy in Villa's raid. He had purchased arms from a manufacturer in Columbus, prior to president Wilson's arms embargo against the Villistas during the Mexican Revolution.

According to one oldtimer I interviewed, who was involved in the raid, the arms that Villa had purchased turned out to be duds. The interviewee, Lauro Trevizo, claimed that the Villistas discovered the sad truth about the arms in the heat of battle:

"The bullets exploded without going anywhere," he said, as we drank coffee in his humble adobe dwelling in the town of Namiquipa, which happens to be one of the places where the Pershing Punitive Expedition went through in its futile search for Villa.

Whether legitimate or not, Villa's attack on Columbus was to indelibly stamp this town with its weird identity.

By the way, for those who love kids until they become teenagers, Columbus is an ideal place. It has a pre-school and elementary school but no junior high or high school.

Non-Mainstream Entertainment (2 of 5 pts)

Columbus is a true-to-life Pancho Villa theme park, with none of the commercial distortions typical of those planned environments. One can reenact the battle, with several of the original structures still standing. The Columbus Historical Museum, for example, is housed in the old railroad depot.

For tracing the path of Pershing's Punitive Expedition, a free map is available. Years ago, I did this; in an old Chevy, I bounced across unmarked, packed-dirt ranch roads, finding two more participants in the 1916 attack (both long-since deceased), plus a 95-year old Villista, General Nicolas Fernandez. Fernandez explained why Pershing never located Villa. While Villa hid in a cave, Fernandez led Pershing on a wild goose chase. He did so by traveling from town to town with a covered wagon, telling the locals that Villa was inside the wagon recovering from a wound.

When Pershing's men trekked through the same places, modern human rights ideas were out of style and extraordinary methods were used to force people to talk. Naturally, the people pointed in the direction of Fernandez' empty covered wagon.

Ol' Nicolas might have made up the story, but judging by the incredible wealth of details, many later corroborated through other sources, he was telling it like a straight shooter.

In the state park, among extensive cactus gardens, visitors may view a short film on Villa in the old 1902 customs house.

TOTAL POINTS: 18

DOWNTOWN LOS ANGELES, CALIFORNIA

os Angeles, California has two downtowns side by side. On the west is the developers' downtown, with modern skyscrapers containing hotels, banks and insurance companies. It's an austere, sanitized neighborhood. Often there are entire blocks where the eyes meet dark glass or stone with no visible sign of commerce. The streets are dead. In fact, most of these buildings are reached exclusively by car, via underground garage.

The other downtown, to the east, past various "social boundaries" that separate it psychically from the west, is Los Angeles' Third World downtown. According to articles in *The Los Angeles Times*, developer Ira Yellin has suddenly become a visionary and is planning a "Grand Central Square" project at Broadway and 3rd Street as a catalyst to create "a funky residential district akin to Greenwich Village." He has private and public backers.

The only problem is, downtown L.A. is already funky, thanks to the Mexicans, other Latin Americans, and smaller contingents of Asians and African Americans. Writer Alexander Cockburn refers to the tackier and more colorful bazaars which make Broadway the busiest such retail thoroughfare north of Mexico City.

"Unlike many cities," he adds, "Los Angeles has preserved most of its 1900-1925 Beaux-Arts commercial core, a fossil Downtown revived in recent years as the retail center of the Spanish-speaking inner city."

The banks fled this area and went east when they witnessed the influx of Latin Americans, figuring the place would then become a wasteland. "Instead," Cockburn observes, "these are the liveliest blocks in the whole Downtown."

Mixed-Use Zoning (1 of 4 pts)

Presently, the few residences in this vibrant downtown are fleabag hotels. That could change, possibly for the better, possibly for the worse, when Yellin's project is completed.

"Broadway can eventually become a real city walk," he said, referring to the theme-parkish Universal Studios' "City Walk." While he is right in suggesting that the so-called City Walk is phony, he is presumptuous in putting down the city walk that already exists on Broadway and vicinity.

Alternative Economy (3 pts)

The question is, can his plan succeed without pushing out the very people who bring life to the neighborhood? The intention is to include apartments above the first-floor commerce, ranging from subsidized units for low- and moderate-income residents to market rate.

In theory it sounds great, but what will happen when he refurbishes the 78-year-old Grand Central Market, arguably this country's most exciting open-air food bazaar? As it is now, the Grand Central Market "survived and even thrived as one of the few truly urban places left in Los Angeles." Its stalls and shops serve food, groceries and sundry items and it is "as eclectic as its clientele from—lawyers to bums."

My wife and I used to shop at the Central Market because of its bargain prices and its multicultural atmosphere. It reminds me of La

Merced in Mexico City in the same way that Broadway reminds me of Mexico's bustling San Juan de Letrán Avenue. These are places, in both L.A. and Mexico City, where people of limited resources can get a business going.

If the place is "refurbished," will these folks be priced out of it and replaced by a more upscale group of vendors? And if this happens, will the produce prices zoom up?

The alternate economy of Downtown L.A. is not limited to Central Market and Broadway. A few blocks south and a block or so east is the garment district, where one can purchase new clothing for half the price in warehouses and funky shops.

Public Hangouts (2 of 5 pts)

Central Market also has rough-hewn food-and-drink stalls where one can sip beer or coffee, eat tacos and other homemade fast foods, while sitting on old wooden stools. If you want to move up a few rungs in furnishings, try the historic Clifton's Cafeteria, within walking distance, where downtown regulars congregate. Clifton's is large, but with a cozy atmosphere.

Here and there are a few other ragtag spots to sit down, nurture a beverage and watch a dazzling array of humanity.

Pedestrian Friendly (4 pts)

One of the reasons for the renewed developer interest in downtown is the proximity of the Metro Red Line. As it was, Latinos found it easy to bus into downtown since their neighborhoods are right on the periphery. Traffic and parking was hassle enough to discourage people from more distant neighborhoods from coming into this part of downtown. But with the Metro, residents from more outlying neighborhoods can now get out at the Pershing Square Station and everything will be within a few blocks.

The streets are teeming with people of all different walks of life and cultures, with the Spanish language as the primary chorus. But the buildings, too, challenge and please the eyes. Yellin's property, for example, includes the Bradbury Building, deservedly listed on the National Register of Historic Places.

According to Cockburn, the Bradbury Building is a "famous old utopian socialist structure whose architect followed the instructions of his dead brother via Ouija board."

Non-Mainstream Entertainment (2 of 5 pts)

Along Broadway are a number of baroque movie houses, including the one in Yellin's 12-story Million Dollar Building. The Million Dollar Theatre is Mexican-Los Angeles' version of New York's Radio City Music Hall, offering Spanish-language variety and floor shows, movies and bingo. The product being sold is nostalgia for Mexico (and sometimes Central America).

My Mexican friends find it comical that back in Mexico, it is announced that such-and-such entertainer will be performing in the United States, when in reality, the performance, in the Million Dollar Theatre, is a virtual extension of Mexico.

Perhaps the greatest show of downtown, maybe the greatest show on earth if we are to believe the tabloids, is a block west of Broadway and a couple of blocks north on Hill Street. In the Municipal, Superior and Federal Courts, you can sit in on the steady flow of sensational trials that the City of Los Angeles offers in order to "outperform" neighboring Hollywood.

Cross-Cultural (5 pts)

While Latin Americans are largely responsible for a vital downtown economy (Broadway surpasses Rodeo Drive in sales), I found that there are people from numerous ethnic and cultural backgrounds who visit or hang out in Downtown L.A.

As can be expected, people of middle-class background who have not been exposed to these cultures may harbor a subjective fear that this downtown is not safe. But according to Donald F. McIntyre, President of the Central City Association of L.A., "Los Angeles has one of the safest downtowns of any major U.S. city according to FBI crime statistics."

I've seen some pretty seedy characters late night in Downtown L.A., but my subjective experience tells me it is much safer than other apparently less menacing L.A. neighborhoods.

Ironically, wealthy Angelinos will spend large sums of money on visits to developing countries while never taking a short excursion into the east side of Downtown L.A., and the surrounding neighborhoods, where the various Third World countries come together.

Another irony: on the north part of downtown is L.A.'s version of Williamsburg. Olvera Street is what everyone would like Mexico to be. It's a type of Mexico theme park, created a quarter of a century ahead of Disneyland. Beyond Olvera Street's authentic, handmade tortillas, the real "campesino" and "proletario" Mexico is on the streets of Downtown L.A. and in several surrounding neighborhoods.

Upended Facilities (1 of 3 pts)

Just east of downtown is an industrial area with abandoned factories where various artists, one of them a sculptor friend of ours, have moved in and refurbished. Unexpectedly, this neighborhood has not become another Soho, perhaps in part because one must pass through a massive and depressing skid row area to get here from downtown.

Positive-Expectation Gambling (2 pts)

Another block west of Hill is Olive Street, where you can hop on an express bus to Santa Anita, widely considered the prettiest race track in the United States. During early morning betting, visitors more aesthetically inclined can eat an outdoor breakfast at Clockers' Corner, sitting among horse owners and trainers, and watch the horses work out with the rugged San Gabriel Mountains in the background. If hangouts had ratings, this one would get five stars.

When Santa Anita is closed, some of the best thoroughbreds, riders and trainers van south to Hollywood Park, in nearby Inglewood. Both tracks offer simulcasts of Northern California races as well.

Freedom of the Bedroom (2 pts)

Meanwhile, the City of Los Angeles has passed every possible law to prohibit discrimination based on sexual orientation. L.A. is the home of the hour- and two-hour motel rooms, at reduced rates, of course. Since the turnover at these places is sometimes high, lunch hour quickies and such, if you're thinking of using the facility, make sure they've changed the sheets.

It has become a cliché to put down Los Angeles for its voracious expansion into outlandish suburbs with virtually identical mini-malls every half mile along the primary thoroughfares. But Downtown L.A. is a real city. While the Metro is at least a half-century late in coming, it should eventually bring more people into downtown, combined with less traffic.

It seems unlikely that the development plans of the future will overgentrify the downtown. But please, don't convert Central Market into an upscale food mall.

In some ways it is easier to write objectively about places that I visit strictly for purposes of research. Perhaps I am too attached to this section of town for an objective rating; for a number of years, I worked, shopped and hung out in the Third World side of Downtown Los Angeles. It is an exciting place, one of the few spots in the whole city where you do better on foot than in a car.

TOTAL POINTS: 22

EL PASO/JUAREZ, TEXAS, MEXICO

hile dusty, sprawling El Paso will never win a beauty contest, this is arguably the most electrifying city in the United States, with help from Juarez, a quarterback sneak away.

A large number of the combined 1.7 million inhabitants have business associates, friends and relatives on both sides of the border.

Cross-Cultural (5 pts)

You can probably tell these twins apart more easily than the pair to the north (Minneapolis-St.Paul), even though El Paso is over 70 percent Mexican/Mexican-American. "Meanwhile," writes Jimmy Breslin, "slowly, El Paso becomes the first Mexican city under the American flag."

A small population of African Americans is integrated within the city, and marketable arts and crafts have led to the rebirth of the nearby Tigua (or Tiwa) Indians.

If that's not enough, the campus of the University of Texas at El Paso is done up in Tibetan Revival architecture, lifted from designs in *National Geographic* after a 1916 fire destroyed almost half the campus. The three oldest buildings were copied from a Tibetan monastery and fortress.

But the true dynamism of the place is the interaction of so-called First and Third Worlds, questionable terms that we use here simply because they've become accepted jargon.

Pedestrian Friendly (2 of 4 pts)

Consider El Paso's core. If this city had fit in with the trend, its downtown would have been weakened economically and socially as the population sprawled out into suburbs. But being right at the border, the downtown is a magnet for the daily infusion of Mexican shoppers (while at the same time, American shoppers cross the other way). This phenomenon has kept the downtown vibrant and viable.

"There are still small, family-operated hotels, as in the old cities, with little coffee shops," says Debbie Nathan, El Paso resident and author of *Women and Other Aliens* (Cinco Puntos Press), a book about the U.S.-Mexican border.

There are real businesses and schlocky shops with flashy merchandise, good bakeries and lots of Mexican food, tasty and cheap.

For Debbie, it's a ten-minute walk to downtown from her Sunset Heights neighborhood, and she can even walk it across the border. Thanks to the survival of downtown, peripheral neighborhoods like hers and Central El Paso remain inviting places to live in. Sunset Heights itself is a vigorous mix of yuppified mansions and blue collar renters in old Victorian houses.

Meanwhile, a chain of mountains seemingly lost its way and settled incongruously in the middle of town. Debbie's husband is fond of climbing them. From some of the peaks is a panorama of two countries in spirited interaction.

Non-Mainstream Entertainment (4 of 5 pts)

City mountain climbing is but one form of bizarre recreation. Author Tom Miller (*On The Border*) observes people with binoculars watching the Border Patrol in action, a presentation of living theater. From the Mexican side, folks can watch the Border patrol watch them: a binocular duel.

Then there are the raunchy bars/dance halls on both sides of the border, where you can hear "Norteña conjuntos," bands with accordions, bass and guitar which play rhythmic Tex-Mex music, influenced by the Spanish "paso doble" and the Polish polka. This genre of music is part of an oral culture that used to function (and still does sometimes) as a regional newspaper, recounting news about crimes and love affairs and revolutions.

It is also the Mexican equivalent of the blues, especially in its slower "ranchera" form.

(During troubled times, I used to go dancing in these bars as a therapeutic escape from a dark tunnel I had dug for myself.)

Transvestite bars and government-regulated whorehouses across the border add another dimension to the entertainment scene. While many of the prostitutes are accomplished actresses, the truth is that it is strictly a business, nurtured by the lack of economic opportunity, according to Daniela, a prostitute I was able to interview during a business slowdown.

I invited her to a drink and she shook her head, "sssh," whispering that I shouldn't waste my money, that the bartender would serve her a Coke and charge me for a Rum and Coke. She explained the nature of her livelihood.

"When I'm working, I don't feel a thing," she said, matter-of-factly. "I just act it out for the money. I reserve my pleasure for my boyfriend."

Public Hangouts (4 of 5 pts)

The city of Juarez is one extended public hangout. El Paso has a central Plaza, with its regulars, as well as bars, hotel coffee shops and informal Mexican restaurants.

Upended Facilities (1 of 3 pts)

An added nuance to the ambience is an old brewery, now converted into an apartment complex where many artists reside.

Alternative Economy (2 of 3 pts)

It used to be that an informal economy spilled over the border on both sides. Lots of street vendors, contraband and more surreptitious stuff. It remains to be seen whether the North American Free Trade Agreement will temper this action.

U.S. citizens can buy groceries and produce in Mexico at about 60 percent of cost; less-expensive dentistry and car repair is also available. Prices are volatile, as Mexico usually suffers massive devaluation of the peso about every six years, which is the term of its president.

Meanwhile, small, downtown El Paso businesses have survived the regional mall phenomenon thanks to Juarez residents and tourists from across the border.

Bizarre Geography (4 of 6 pts)

The mountains in the middle of town and Mexico to the south are just the beginning of El Paso's unique geographic position. This city is isolated from the rest of Texas. It is closer to Chihuahua City in Mexico than to Austin, Texas. Geographically it should be part of New Mexico but a buffer zone of uninhabited desert keeps that state farther off than the map would suggest.

Although El Paso's altitude makes it a little milder than the rest of Texas, it still gets mighty hot during the summer. Residents can find an escape up in New Mexico's mountains, and during the winter, they can ski at Ruidoso, New Mexico.

The breathtaking Copper Canyon, with its spectacular winding train ride over bottomless gorges, makes the Grand Canyon seem shallow in comparison, and is within a one-shot drive south from El Paso to Chihuahua.

Then there is the bizarre human geography that sees North Americans crossing over to live in Juarez and Mexicans coming up to live in El Paso.

Independent Politics (1 of 3 pts)

Unfortunately, a wedge is forced into this dynamic cross-cultural situation periodically by anti-immigrant sentiment, usually provoked by opportunistic politicians. According to Texas writer Molly Ivins, "When Texas's economy was in a slump in the mid-'80s, immigrant bashing was a politically profitable game here...Of course, no one has ever been able to claim that anyone immigrated to Texas in order to take advantage of our generous (ahem) welfare benefits or health care for the poor (in those days, we let 'em die outside public clinics if they didn't have the 75 bucks)."

At this writing, the Clinton administration has revived the border hysteria with a blockade. As a result, according to Susan Kern, member of the El Paso Border Rights Coalition, "brown skinned school kids with gym bags were likely to be stopped by the Border Patrol."

In response, El Paso's Bowie High School filed a suit against the Border Patrol. Meanwhile, Texas's Bishop Pena joined other southwest U.S. bishops in seeking a suspension of the blockade, alleging that the Immigration and Naturalization blockade has hurt families on both sides of the border.

Debbie Nathan is also a member of the El Paso Border Rights Coalition. Nathan suggests, in an article in *The Nation*, that precisely at the time that Latin Americans crossing into the States are being blamed for El Paso's low wages and high unemployment, "dozens of Fortune 500 companies have plants in the area. The catch is that they're in Juarez, and they pay 72 cents an hour."

Nathan adds: "Border control, one of Bill Clinton's obsessions, is free trade's deepest irony: the fact that while greenbacks can go anywhere in the world, wetbacks can't."

But El Pasoans, pondering thoughtful solutions, have formed a citywide group of community leaders that has proposed making Juarez and El Paso a free immigration zone and even combining the school systems. According to Nathan, "this binational vision would require careful nurturing, in part because of deep currents of resentment against immigrants that run through the community psyche" in spite of the fact that the city is nearly 70 percent Mexican-American.

In El Paso, "free radicals" have nothing to do with biology. They are people attracted to the lively city, who stay to work on causes, such as immigration, only to get burned out. "El Paso is acutely addicting," says Kern, with its "love-hate excitement, but the cost is cynicism. We have a thriving community of mobile activists."

Cleaning up the river and stopping nuclear waste storage are other issues that catalyze large contingents of independent activists, but El Paso is a tough place to win a struggle, when you consider the powerful multinational interest groups along with a vulnerable local workforce whose next check is not a sure thing.

Jimmy Breslin has written, "El Paso is the most exciting place I know in this country." Will the Blockade dampen this crosscultural exhilaration? Probably not. No recent immigration legislation has managed to stop the flow of history, and the twin cities of El Paso-Juarez have too much to lose by going their separate ways.

TOTAL POINTS: 27

(With Sunland Race Track in El Paso and off-track-betting covering all major U.S. tracks in Juarez, the point total includes the 2 points within the "positive-expectation gambling" category. Furthermore, El Paso earns 2 bonus points...the Mexican-U.S. border is the only place in the world where First and Third World cities meet, and El Paso and Juarez are the most interactive pair of cities along that border.)

ELKO, NEVADA

Elko, Nevada is the proud host of the Annual Cowboy Poetry Gathering and the current site of what may be the last gold rush in the continental USA, one of the first high-tech gold rushes, using a complicated leaching process to extract microscopic gold from huge ore deposits.

Unconventional Regional Customs (3 of 6 pts)

Elko may be the only small town in the USA with a full-service airline. The Casino Express brings people back and forth from places like Waterloo and Fort Dodge, Iowa, and Akron, Colorado. The airline fills a small-town-to-small-town void in the air travel economy, triggered by the casino hotels in Elko.

And perhaps a lucky cowboy poet might be in one of the places serviced by Casino Express and not have to travel first to a hub, in order to get to Elko.

Held the last weekend of January, when ranch folks are most likely to be free from their duties, the Cowboy Poetry Gathering requires participants to be engaged in ranching or working on ranches and requires an audition. Cowboys (a term that is also used for cowgirls) are selected from as many states as possible.

More than 8,000 people attend the event, which is held at several venues, including a museum, a convention center, and the Western Folklife Building, a converted hotel.

"It's like a family reunion," one of the founders noted, "only everyone likes each other."

Non-Mainstream Entertainment (1 of 5 pts)

In fact, Elko was once referred to as "America's last cow town," and the obligatory brothels help complete that description. There are about eight of them in Elko, where, as in most counties of Nevada, prostitution is legal.

Cross-Cultural (2 of 5 pts)

The mysterious Basque culture is a mainstay in town and in the surrounding country. No one really knows the origin of the twangy and complex Basque language, which has nothing in common with the romance languages found at the Spain-France border where the Basques come from.

In Elko there are four good Basque restaurants, as well as several local businesses owned by Basques. Elko General Merchandise goes back three generations of Basques and you can hear the language spoken in the store. Once a general store, today it mainly deals in clothing for ranchers and laborers.

Elko proudly celebrates the annual National Basque Festival every Fourth of July Weekend.

The cowboy culture was originally Hispanic and lots of Latins work on ranches, so recent poetry gatherings give ample attention to Hispanic cowboys.

Public Hangouts (3 of 5 pts)

Elko is brimming with public hangouts for all generations, including Machis, a pub restaurant, and D'Orazios, an Italian restaurant, formerly a Mediterranean style house.

Upended Facilities (1 of 3 pts)

D'Orazio's conversion makes sense from a Mediterranean perspective, but there are other odder transformations. For example, what is now the police station was once the old Mormon Church, and the Western Folklife Building is found in a former hotel. An old Pony Express cabin is on display downtown.

Pedestrian Friendly (2 of 4 pts)

The vast distances of western USA do not lend themselves to pedestrian culture, and Elko County alone is larger than Massachusetts, Rhode Island, Connecticut and Delaware combined!

Nevertheless, there's a good feel to being on foot; Elko is a small town with big city excitement. Beyond the glitzy casinos are a number of classical houses from the turn-of-the century to the 1920s, and most downtown buildings are at least fifty years old. The Star Hotel dates back to 1910. The Telescope (1908), may be the oldest structure now used for a bowling alley.

Positive-Expectation Gambling (2 pts)

Two of the casinos, The Red Lion and Stockman's, have race and sports books, and several others are thinking of following the trend. Poker rooms are available in all the casinos.

Cowboy poetry is but one of the reasons for the perception that anything is possible in Elko. "Immigrants" from California and other parts of the U.S. are settling in the area, partly drawn in by the gold rush, but also attracted by the open spaces.

The rugged, snow-covered Ruby Mountain range is a majestic sight, towering over Elko from the distance. The landscape is typical stark Nevada, but with a healthy high altitude climate.

Some controversy has surrounded the mines, since federal lands are ceded to mining companies for a few pennies thanks to an antiquated 1882 law. The Department of the Interior is trying to change the law in order to collect royalties on minerals that are being removed from taxpayer lands.

And the environmental consequences of the gold rush? Who cares that there's a huge hole in the scenery in the form of a massive pit mine, says one company representative. "You're not talking about Yosemite."

For most folks here, jobs are more important than scenery, but local ranchers worry that the mines' "dewatering" processes could disrupt the water table.

TOTAL POINTS: 14

ELY, NEVADA

Ely is the largest town in a 100-mile radius of the stark, unfor-giving Nevada desert, gateway to a stretch of Route 50 la-beled as "the loneliest road in America." Visitors centers along Route 50 offer travelers a free Highway 50 Survival Kit.

Unconventional Regional Customs (2 of 6 pts)
Dotted along that road are "communities" of one or two mobile homes, often with a rusty gas pump and piles of would-be construction materials, a last frontier to American homesteaders.

"We wouldn't be here if we weren't rugged individualists," responded one Ely resident, when I asked him about the loners out there on the desert. Some people thrive on vastness and solitude.

Non-Mainstream Recreation (6 pts)
From a non-judgmental, "social" perspective, it makes sense that the bar-bordello, a fixture of the Old West, survives in the vast solitude of Nevada. Prostitution is legal and regulated by the State. According to National Geographic, Ely has The Big 4, portrayed as "a legal bar and bordello," whose "owner, Mel Clifton, belongs to the Chamber of Commerce and has sponsored the little league."

There are three brothels remaining on the once-boisterous "Bronc Alley," appearing today much like neighborhood bars. "Licensed by the city, the girls are independent contractors" who "keep a low profile in town."

The bordello may not be the kinkiest place in the region. The nearby wilderness is a haven for rockhounders. The Ely region is to rocks what France is to wines.

There are quartz-family minerals, usually agates and jaspers, often appearing as petrified wood. There is fire opal, a valuable stone, and chrysocolla, jade, rhyolite, variscite, obsidian and garnet. Get lucky and you might find gold.

Permission may be obtained to rockhound on private lands. Rockhounders are advised to fill excavation holes for the protection of livestock, and to take home only what can be used. It's a no-no to collect in parks. Public lands are subject to mining claims. Mining claims can be recognized by four foot tall, 4x4 claim posts. The law states that collecting on public lands must not be "for the purpose of sale or barter." If you stumble upon a dinosaur fossil, you should stop digging and report it to the Bureau of Land Management.

The back country has its dangers. Sensible precautions include taking high boots and a snakebite kit, although a snakebite is now rare. Since the best rockhounding sites are off on unpaved roads, two vehicles are suggested, in case one of them fails. Also, watch out for abandoned mine shafts.

The Ely area is particularly rich in garnets. From Ely, take U.S. 50 east to the Ruth turn-off (Nev. 44) and take the dirt road on the right, less than a mile up canyon. Dirt trails lead south over Garnet Hill. Garnets may be found by breaking up the pinkish rhyolite where they were formed in quartz vugs. The best luck is reported by rockhounders who have searched the light-colored soil for dark spots which turn out to be reddish crystals, weathered from the rock through the centuries. Ely garnets are a deep red variety. The supply is inexhaustible once you look hard enough.

If you like traveling back in time, there are other places of interest. Cave Lake State Park is perched 7,500 feet up in the Schell Creek Range, with fishing, camping, boating, and hiking. Go 8 miles south of Ely, on Route 50, then 7 miles on the unpaved Success Summit Road.

The Ward Charcoal Ovens State Monument represents a rare example of American architecture. Six 30-foot high, beehive-shaped stone ovens were built in 1876 to provide fuel for nearby smelters: 15 miles south of Ely on 50, then 6 miles by dirt road.

The Nevada Northern Railway Museum, 11th Street and Avenue A, a turn-of-the-century railroad complex, is described as the best preserved short line railroad in the world. During summers, you can take rides on the old steam engine train. For $100, you can drive the steam engine around the yard for an hour, accompanied by an expert. Exhibits include a 1907 depot, a roundhouse, antique work equipment and lots of rolling stock.

About 75 miles west of Ely is the enclave of Eureka, a 19th century mining town, including a courthouse, theater, newspaper office, all of which date back to 1879. Other less-preserved ghost towns dot the harsh terrain. In Osceola, kinky prospectors still look for the mother lode.

Positive-Expectation Gambling (1 of 2 pts)
Avoid the bad-bet slot machines. Only the Hotel Nevada has black jack.

Upended Facilities (1 of 3 pts)
Culinary S&M: Cell block dining at the Jailhouse Motel and Dining Hall. To lock into your reservation, phone 702/289-3033.

Because of the high altitudes of the region, the summer climate is less hostile than the neighboring furnace of Las Vegas.

TOTAL POINTS: 10

EUREKA SPRINGS, ARKANSAS OZARKS

In Eureka Springs, Arkansas, there is one downtown building that has three different addresses. None of the town's 238 streets ever cross at right angles. An old church building has its entrance through the bell tower.

Bizarre Geography (5 of 6 pts)
The reason for these idiosyncrasies is that the early settlers constructed in unreasonable places. In a setting where hundreds of feet of elevation sometimes separate one street from another, it is no wonder that *National Geographic* writer Mel White describes the map of the city as looking "like a plate of spaghetti."

In a town made up primarily of steep hillsides, from which 42 natural springs flow, one should not be surprised by all the hairpin turns, nor by the total absence of traffic signals.

Unconventional Regional Customs (3 of 6 pts)
It is to be expected that such a preposterous place would attract a large contingent of artists. In fact, the blending of the early Ozark settlers and the immigrant artists has led to what White calls a "hillbilly cosmopolitanism."

As a result, local residents are usually entertained rather than appalled by each other's eccentricities.

Naturally, in such a captivating setting, tourist entrepreneurs eventually took over. There were positive and negative results. The good news was that a profusion of pastel Victorian gingerbred residences, stone buildings with native limestone walls and old stone sidewalks were preserved as a visual feast. The bad news is that many tacky tourist attractions sprang up.

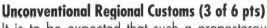

The human consequences of the tourist trade have led to the odd custom of working extra shifts during the tourist season and then taking protracted vacations sometimes extending from mid-autumn through early spring.

The weird geography has acted as a magnet for other bizarre types of people. For example, Eureka Springs hosts an annual conference for UFO investigators every April.

Pedestrian Friendly (4 pts)

The jagged, asymmetrical terrain has engendered still another attractive feature. The automobile, twentieth-century deity, suffers a de facto exclusion from the town. The streets are too narrow for parking and with the sharp turns, a sauntering pedestrian would outpace a motor vehicle.

In place of automobiles, convenient trolleys and open-air trams make for pleasant transportation. But strolling is the best way to enjoy the town. Eureka Springs functions as an open-air art maze, with the walker in no hurry to find a way out.

Public Hangouts (2 of 5 pts)

When it's time to stop strolling and sit down for awhile, there are a number of cafés and parks. During the tourist season, these spots probably lose some of their atmosphere. According to one resident I interviewed, "We like the tourists, but you should be here in the off season. Then, the artists come into the cafés more regularly. Winter is the time to get to know people. That's when everybody gets to know each other again."

Mixed-Use Zoning (2 of 4 pts)

For half the year, Eureka Springs is a mixed-use town, with no way to segregate residence and commerce. During the high season, the residential flavor of the town is eclipsed by tourist trade.

Alternative Economy (1 of 3 pts)

One would think that the abundance of established tourism would seal the fate of marginal folk, but there are voids for non-mainstream types. There are street musicians, for example, and a couple of "starving artist fairs" each year. Street vending is not an intrinsic custom because the streets are simply too narrow.

While a few tourist attractions may seem awkwardly superimposed on a town that doesn't really need them, Eureka Springs also has a steady stream of festivals with inherent connections to the setting, most notably the early-autumn Ozark Folk Festival, diverse arts-and-crafts fairs and a summer blues festival. In early December, the Preservation Society opens the doors of many of the town's seductive homes for public tours.

Tourism or no, Eureka Springs is not planning to straighten out its enticing asymmetry, which provides an ideal context for all kinds of eccentric people.

TOTAL POINTS: 17

GENESEE COUNTY, NEW YORK

ust across the county line from Attica, site of the famous prison rebellion and subsequent State-initiated massacre, is Genesee County, New York. Like most prisons across the country, Attica is overcrowded. But the jails in neighboring Genesee County have so much room to spare that the federal corrections system is sending inmates to Genesee. Housing these inmates brought in $630,000 to county coffers in 1993 alone.

Just what is the Genesee justice system doing that nearby counties and other states are not?

Unconventional Regional Customs (6 pts)

The answer is found in a justice system that views itself as peacemaker and healer and that involves the whole community in its functions. While demagogues around the country tell us that it is either the victims' rights or the criminals' rights, the Genesee formula combines a sensitivity to victims' rights unheard of in other jurisdictions, with a parallel belief that alternatives to incarceration should be employed whenever feasible.

Victims are kept apprised of the status of the case against the offender, and helped in the preparation of a "victim impact statement," which the judge takes into account in the sentencing process.

Victims are also given the option of confronting the perpetrator. Occasionally, reconciliation takes place, but simply getting the anger out and directing it at the person who caused it is part of the healing process. Whenever possible, perpetrators are ordered to compensate the victim.

The victims' participation in the sentencing also adds to the wisdom of the system, according to Dennis Wittman, the coordinator of the Community Service and Victim Assistance programs. "We've seen many criminal cases, even violent ones, in which victim-directed sentencing turns out to be community-based sentencing. Genesee Justice has proven that when they're attended to, victims want safety and accountability and responsibility from

the offender, not vengeance."

This allows a greater chance for offenders to recognize the human impact of their crime. It also gives offenders a chance to seek forgiveness.

The Genesee County philosophy is that the offender's first obligation is to make amends with the victim and the community. When an offender shows a strong interest in making amends, he or she is given the opportunity to make restitution and to be reaccepted into the community.

A tightly monitored plan is presented to the victim, district attorney and defense lawyer, customized to the nature of the offense and the victim's recommendations, as well as to the input of the community. If the offender follows the plan, charges may be reduced or dropped; if the offender fails to follow the plan, the case will revert to normal court proceedings.

The outcome of this system is a weird combination: greater satisfaction of victims along with less jail time for offenders.

Lest one think this is the scheme of bleeding heart liberals, Genesee County is a conservative place and the program only works because the whole community is involved.

Community service is thus treated quite seriously and "not as a way to let offenders off easily," Wittman adds. Community members volunteer as community sponsors of offenders who are trying to make amends, with 107 nonprofit agencies and 80 volunteer sponsors participating. Meanwhile, there are 90 volunteers who work with crime victims, and the victim's concerns are attended to for as long as it takes.

This community involvement also allows for judges to come up with tailor-made sentences that relate to the crime instead of the across-the-board mandatory sentences.

Only 6 percent of those who have received community-service sentences have either failed to complete their sentence or been rearrested.

Aside from the "rent" money the County makes from its empty jail rooms, it has saved millions of dollars resulting from the days that offenders were not incarcerated.

Dennis Wittman estimates it has cost the county an average of $350 per case that has been handled in the diversion program, cases that would have cost anywhere from $14,000 to $25,000 per year had they resulted in incarceration.

Alternative Economy (1 of 3 pts)

The Genesee justice solution must be seen in context. When heavy industry moved out, an industrial center was created, a type of semi-cooperative of approximately 50 small businesses. These in turn were linked to vocational training programs and an apprentice system in the freshman year of high school. Thus, the economic infrastructure so vital in crime prevention acts as a support to the criminal justice system.

The area is also a fertile agricultural basin and a farmers market hits town two or three times a week.

Mixed-Use Zoning (3 of 4 pts)

The downtown area of Batavia, the county seat, is still an active place, although it now has to contend with a Wal-Mart. The town leaders made what one resident told me was a big mistake with an urban renewal project on one side of Main Street. But on the other side, as if the town literally had a split personality, older structures of greater character were renovated.

People still live in various apartments above the downtown stores, and residential streets are one block either way off Main Street. Housing for seniors is found in the commercial area, as well as a youth center, which makes for a nice mix of generations.

Upended Facilities (1 of 3 pts)

The old firehouse is a restaurant and an old factory has been converted into an office building.

Positive-Expectation Gambling (2 pts)

Batavia Downs Raceway is the oldest pari-mutuel track in the country. If you prefer thoroughbreds over the harness races, Finger Lakes Race Track is less than an hour away.

Conservative Genesee County is not a newcomer to its revolutionary justice systems. It was an integral part of the Underground Railroad, and the town of Elba, not far from Batavia, has private homes from that period that are still connected by tunnels.

TOTAL POINTS: 13

HARPERS FERRY, WEST VIRGINIA

When the National Park Service moved into Harpers Ferry, two possible ominous futures loomed ahead. First there was the potential of converting a picturesque small town into a theme park, and then the prospect that locals might become second class citizens, eclipsed by the dramatic history of their forebears.

Neither of these futures came to be. While the National Park Service could not totally avoid "strained relations" with the townfolk, the recent 50th anniversary of the "park" was organized through a partnership between residents and park employees.

Ironically, what elevates Harpers Ferry above other historical parks is its double function as an American small town and a living historical monument. The Park Service functions in such a subtle way that visitors would be hard pressed to draw a boundary between the current town and the preserved historical structures.

Unconventional Regional Customs (2 of 6 pts)

 Like Columbus, New Mexico, Harpers Ferry owes its identity to the man who assaulted it, in this case, abolitionist John Brown. John Brown was executed in nearby Charles Town, five miles down the road. Robert E. Lee oversaw the proceedings that led to his death. Thoreau and Emerson protested the execution. John Wilkes Booth was in charge of the hanging.

John Brown did not enter martyrdom alone. Most of his nineteen sons were involved in the raid on Harpers Ferry. Many of them died along with their father.

The history of the town comes alive within the original buildings and ruins that existed at the time of the raid. Although Brown was condemned as an outlaw, he maintained that the crimes of slavery could not be purged without blood. Sixteen months after his execution, the Civil War broke out and his historical vision was corroborated.

Bizarre Geography (5 of 6 pts)

The town of Harpers Ferry could be mistaken for a fantastic model railroad set-up. Located on a cliff jutting out between the upper arms of a letter Y formed by the spectacular confluence of the Shenandoah and Potomac Rivers, the town is gilded on both sides by old railroad trestles, one still in use.

Its early-and mid-19th century red brick buildings merge with the unique shale bedrock, so that natural and human construction blends asymmetrically. The harpers shale that is featured in numerous village walls and outdoor stairways is unique to the region.

This same bedrock can be seen shining as it crops out of the clear Potomac and Shenandoah waters. When the rivers are low, one looks down upon a collage of bedrock formations.

The Blue Ridge Mountains in the background complete the dreamscape, with freight and passenger trains leaving the town over a trestle that disappears into a dark tunnel, beneath a cliff dotted with rock climbers.

The base of town has been flooded dramatically on numerous occasions. In places where buildings were washed away, you can still see the drill bit marks in the shale walls.

Snuggling in a sliver between Maryland and Virginia, Harpers Ferry looks much like the town in the classic childrens' book, *The Little Engine That Could.*

Pedestrian Friendly (3 of 4 pts)

With shale staircases leading to different levels of the town, Harpers Ferry invites you to walk or hike, then threatens you with ankle-twisting irregularities. In one direction, the pedestrian can cross the town from its base up to its border with Bolivar, an odd, mixed-use "suburb" that has never heard of zoning.

In another direction, past the 1830s St. Peters Catholic Church (within the "park" but not part of it), one heads toward the sky until, suddenly, level ground appears, as if Jack has reached the top of the beanstalk. On this level is a cemetery and the campus of former Storer College.

From every angle there is another view to fill the senses, from restored commercial establishments such as a dry goods store, a confectionary and a blacksmith shop to a pedestrian path along the railroad bridge jutting over the point where the Potomac and Shenandoah meet. Ruins of a mill, an ancient stone bridge and other historic buildings, some restored by the Park Service, others resided in by the locals, complete the picture of this walkers' paradise.

Recent immigrants to Harpers Ferry have been Washington D.C. employees who are tired of the sensory deprivation of the suburbs but want to live away from the city. Excellent train service hauls them back and forth.

Unfortunately the train schedule is only geared to residents. You can go to Harpers Ferry during evening rush hour and you can leave it for Washington, D.C. during the morning rush hour, but otherwise, you need a car to get there, unless you choose to hop a freight. One may arrive at Harpers Ferry by bicycle all the way from Washington via the C&O Canal, which skirts along the Potomac River.

Positive-Expectation Gambling (2 pts)

Nearby Charles Town is a well preserved historical town and home of Charles Town Races, a country track that offers lots of longshots and live simulcast betting from major U.S. tracks. Charles Town Races is noted for its friendly country atmosphere, but economic problems threaten to wipe out the race meetings.

Testifying that Harpers Ferry is the site of living history are a number of families that trace back many generations, including three "free"(unenslaved) African American families dating back to the 1820s.

TOTAL POINTS: 12

HOBOKEN, NEW JERSEY

Threatened with changing times, small cities remain vibrant when they evolve by highlighting those things that made them unique. Big-city consultants are a serious threat to the survival of these cities as "places."

Graffiti from a construction fence in Hoboken, New Jersey:

"WHERE YA FROM?"

"HOBOKEN."

"HOBOKEN? WADDAYA LIVE INNA ABANDONED FACTORY, OR WHAT?"

Hoboken residents had the vision to convert old factories into housing, while preserving, as well, intangible facets of the city's character. According to Father Michael Guglielmelli, O.F.M. CONV, of the Saint Francis Parish, "every block has its own personality. You can fit right in no matter how crazy you are."

 Bizarre Geography (2 of 6 pts)

The physical setting of Hoboken has played an active role in defining the character of the town. The city is packed within a tight grid, a dense, flat place between steep palisades to the west and the lower Manhattan skyline across the Hudson River to the east. Its compactness gives it definition, something the unfocused communities to the north and south don't have.

Within, Hoboken is characterized by its front stoops, iron railings, walkup apartments. Some of its streets are lined with old five-story apartments. Others feature smaller brownstones.

The word "Hoboken" used to be a joke to New Yorkers. It was the quintessential tough industrial-waterfront town. What they didn't know was that Hoboken had originated as a "resort," frequented by personalities such as Alexander Hamilton, Aaron Burr, William Vanderbilt and Horace Greeley.

In the city's industrial stage, when it was known as an Italian city, in its only section of wooden tenements, Frank Sinatra grew up. The Elia Kazan/Arthur Miller/Marlon Brando classic movie, On The Waterfront, was filmed in and about Hoboken. Kazan needed bodyguards to do this film about waterfront corruption. Today, Hoboken's movie career is moving through its John Sayles stage, which represents its evolution from gritty to alternative.

Upended Facilities (3 pts)

Although some gut-and-build urban renewal has taken place near the waterfront, Hoboken officials have emphasized renovation far more than most other cities confronting a parallel dilemma. What are the results of this posture?

In 1976, an abandoned drafting tool factory was saved from demolition; its visionary renovation resulted in the Clock Tower Apartments, 173 large apartments with 12-foot ceilings! Various other ambitious renovations followed.

Mixed-Use Zoning (4 pts)

It remains to be seen whether Hoboken will continue its unpretentious existence. Gentrification, especially near the waterfront, may take its toll on small shops that sport signs in Italian and Spanish (the newest wave of immigrants), while squeezing the locals back toward the palisades.

Meanwhile, no suburban development will ever match the aesthetic value of Hoboken's wrought iron fire escape walk-ups. The five-story row apartments, as exemplified by Washington Street, near 12th, have the old world charm of a Paris "quartier." There are bay windows on some, rounded and sculpted window casing on others reminiscent of Gaudi's Art Nouveau. Windows are not the mere holes in the wall that were created by modernist architects.

There are kinky roof cornices on most Hoboken apartment buildings, rather than utilitarian 90-degree flat corners. But for the air conditioners sticking out of some of those apartments, the scene could have been Parisian.

Other apartment scenes, such as the five-story walkups on Bloomfield Street, between Observer Highway and Newark Street, conjure up Edward Hopper paintings. But most satisfying of all is the fact that commerce has not been excluded from these neighborhoods. Hoboken appears to be all mixed use.

Mixed use means lively streets, but it also has its down side. The big issue today is the outflow of people from the bars. "They're probably good people Monday through Friday," said one resident, "but they can get very rowdy."

Pedestrian Friendly (4 pts)

The city is large enough for roller skaters or walking fanatics to be challenged but compact enough so that everything one needs is within walking distance. The walking is accompanied by a dazzling sensorial display, including spectacular views of the Manhattan skyline, the rocky palisades and bustling neighborhoods.

Noteworthy is the "trompe l'oeil" wall mural on 2nd Street, one short block north of Washington.

One could live quite well here without an automobile. New York City is accessible by railroad, subway, bus and ferry.

Alternative Economy (1 of 3 pts)

Street vending is not an inherent part of the local culture but we did see more than a few stands along Washington Street selling various odds and ends. Ma and pa still have a chance to survive since there is no room for a regional shopping mall.

Public Hangouts (5 pts)

A noteworthy feature of this city is its outdoor café culture. The bars within are graced by homespun elegance, as typified by Miss Kitty's Saloon on Bloomfield Street, just off 1st Street. People are invited to come and experience "surly help, bad food, warm beer and high prices." While the prices were indeed above moderate, the atmosphere was warm and spirited.

The problem with rating evolving places is that you get to see them in one slice of time. We were able to find enough ungentrified spots within to assume that the city can continue to exist in several dimensions. The benches outside the unassuming city hall remained a more proletarian gathering place and at the pizza-deli on Washington at 1st we were able to order real New York pizza by the slice for a reasonable price.

Louise and Jerry's, a cubby-hole place on Washington, attracts old Hobokenites. Yuppies who stray from the other night spots risk being ostracized if they drift into this club.

There's a simmering culture war between residents and partygoers, but with some signs of compromise in sight. A new club owner, Anthony Mastroamauro, typically young, from the Wall Street crowd, happens to be a Hobokenite by birth. It remains to be seen whether entrepreneurs like Mastroamauro can somehow create a bridge between bargoers and long-time residents.

A crafty ordinance allows people to stay in the clubs until 3:00 as long as they've entered prior to 1:00 A.M. Essentially this prevents barhopping, broken bottles and urinating in the street, without cutting away the nightlife.

Cross-Cultural (4 of 5 pts)

Hoboken Farmboy, which specializes in health food, is one of many unmanicured neighborhood stores that might protect the well-preserved town from becoming too upscale for its own good.

According to Sue, longtime resident, Hoboken has lost some of its ethnic character. "The last Italian green grocer is on 1st and

Bloomfield. Fortunately, he has no intention of moving out."

Will the city increasingly lose its multicultural character? we asked. "Ethnic diversity here is second to none," Sue responded. "If it's made in the world, it's sold in Hoboken, particularly cooked and fresh foods. And there are small Hispanic and Asian-run stores all over. Most of the Hispanics are Puerto Ricans."

Positive-Expectation Gambling (2 pts)

The Meadowlands is an easy 10-minute drive, Route 3, west. Pari-mutuel wagering is offered on live racing and simulcasts, with a menu of numerous race tracks, thus allowing bettors to pick and choose their spots according to the best opportunities.

Condominium conversion has been at a standstill, because of infrastructure problems. But in the meantime, apartment rents have skyrocketed, if you are lucky enough to find one. Sue seems to think that the city will survive its gentrification and maintain its ethnic character. "Try Leo's," she says "for its home-cooked Italian food and the best pizza in the world, on 2nd and Grand, and you'll see what I mean."

Father Michael sees it in a positive way. "We've had waves of immigrants, the Dutch, the Italians, the Hispanics. I see the young adults as the newest wave. Now we have the yuppies."

TOTAL POINTS: 25

HOPLAND, CALIFORNIA: "CULINARY WOODSTOCK"

 little more than a month before the nostalgic 1994 Woodstock II celebration, a three-day "culinary Woodstock" took place in and around the little main street USA town of Hopland, California.

Unlike the Woodstock on the other coast, this festival was organized locally. While its noise level was considerably lower than that of Saugerties, New York, Hopland's influence is expected to resound in deceptively muted waves across the country. The tents were there, as were the portable bathrooms, but instead of the mud, there was an impromptu meeting hall and dining room under a big white canopy.

Unconventional Regional Customs (5 of 6 pts)

This festival/retreat represented a manifesto for a movement to grow and cook organic food that is right off the farm rather than trucked from thousands of miles away. The subversives were headed by Fetzer Vineyards, which produces two organically grown wines: Bon Terra, a Chardonay, and a red table wine. Fetzer is striving to become a totally organic farm by the year 2,000.

The other local vineyard, McDowell Valley, defines a similar goal. The influence of these and other local growers has spread to the population in general. McDowell's innovation is a solar-powered plant. Fetzer has a show-case five-acre garden that produces over 1,000 varieties of fruits, vegetables and herbs.

Lest one be left with the notion that this culinary retreat dished out bland health food, it should be noted that restaurant chefs from all over the country converged on this small town of 800 to prepare what Gordon Sinclair, owner of Chicago's Gordon's Restaurant called "the best food I have ever eaten."

Assisting the chefs were members of the local 4-H club.

(Out of sight and range from this revolutionary event is another type of Mendocino County alternative agriculture, hidden in the unmarked woods. With the decline of the lumber industry, marijuana might be one of the county's principal crops. A *New York Times* travel article about the region warns people to avoid the remote wooded areas in that county.)

Alternative Economy (3 pts)

In attendance at the culinary Woodstock, along with town residents, chefs, scientists, restauranteurs, farmers and other children of the sixties, were farmers market organizers from across the country. In other words, aside from the message relating to production (that organic can be feasible economically as well as healthy), the distribution side of the equation was also highlighted. It was manifested that products can and should be sold on a local basis by smaller businesses.

Tiny Hopland was the perfect setting for an event of this magnitude, for it lives and breathes through an alternative, anti-coporate economy. For example, its lively pub, the Hopland Brewery, was the first microbrewery in California since prohibition. Along with its four home-produced ales is an array of good pub food.

The Blue Bird Café, owned by a group of local chefs, has a menu based on organic dishes and orders most of its food from local producers. Then there is Real Goods, a store specializing in energy-saving supplies.

With an economy driven by local producers, in theory residents of the area should no longer suffer the alienation that comes from depending on far-away, faceless corporations. My interviews with various Hopland residents confirmed that a tonality of idealism pervades the town.

Mixed-Use Zoning (2 of 4 pts)

With the 1890 Thatcher Hotel as the Victorian hub of Hopland, there is an eclectic array of structures in and around the three-block long downtown, situated right on Route 101, about 110 miles north of San Francisco. Since it is much easier for a small town to mix residence with commerce, Hopland only gets half the points for this feat. (Real Goods is located in a new building only because the old one burned down.)

Public Hangouts (1 of 5 pts)

Naturally, a small town has no way of competing with places like New Orleans in the realm of public hangouts, but the people we questioned feel very much at home in their café and pub, and that's what makes four walls into a hangout. The valley vineyard setting adds to the intimacy.

Non-Mainstream Recreation (1 of 5 pts)

If you're planning to visit, why not do it in a participatory way. Valley Oaks Garden, part of the Fetzer operation (707/744-1250), offers classes in organic cooking.

TOTAL POINTS: 12

IMPERIAL BEACH, CALIFORNIA

Imperial Beach is the last little beach town in Southern California. If developers had their way, I.B. would go the way of the rest of that coast, ceding to view-blocking condominiums and hotels, driving ma-and-pa businesses inland or out of existence and destroying a way of life.

As I.B.'s residents were rejecting redevelopment in referendums, two Grand Juries were acting as offensive linemen, trying to upend the town's leadership. With no evidence to bring charges, these Grand Juries resorted to writing reports that discredited the residents, citing deficiences such as "no commercial structure of significant size has been built on its undeveloped beaches" since its incorporation in 1956.

Unconventional Regional Customs (4 of 6 pts)

As a result of the victory against the developers, "people here feel real free to be the way they are, even some who just can't quite get the hang of society," according to Jan Hopkins, co-owner of a tiny restaurant on Seacoast Drive called My Little Café. Or, as another resident, John Mahoney once said:

"It welcomes eccentrics. It is a comfort to people who don't have very much but don't feel discriminated against or out of place. It has an absence of pretenses."

One visitor affirms that this town has a "midwestern feel."

When a writer talks about IB's "world-class beach," a local responds: "I'm not sure if he means the mounds of rotting seaweed or the piles of dogshit, which are all a vital part of the scenery, and keep the more squeamish tourists away!"

This independent and primitive spirit may not seem that funky in itself, but in the context of what has happened to the rest of the Southern California coastal "communities," it looks as if the I.B. residents have rejected the easy dollar in order to protect their easy-going lifestyle.

The U.S. National Sand Castle competition draws over 200,000 people in one weekend. When the Port District tried to grab off beach area for development a few years ago, some of the town's "antis" entered the competition, building an elaborate fort with the inscription: "The Port Stops Here." They won first prize.

Bizarre Geography (3 of 6 pts)

At this lattitude, more southerly than notorious frying pans Las Vegas and Phoenix, summers should be unbearable. But the north water currents create the conditions for spring and early fall weather year round; while not far inland, it's sweltering throughout the summer.

"We have relatives 15 miles inland, where it's at least ten to fifteen degrees hotter," says Dottie, an I.B. resident. "We refuse to visit them in the summer."

I.B. touches the border with Tijuana and the fence does not reach the ocean. You can wade or swim back and forth between two countries. Here you'll probably bump into economic refugees, most of whom will soon be caught. Meanwhile, "jet skiing lifeguards often cross the border," Dottie says, "to help out on the other side."

Cross-Cultural (2 of 5 pts)

Being situated on the border allows for a cross-cultural option. You can choose the best or the worst from both worlds. While Tijuana's prices have skyrocketed, there are still bargains across the border in dental care and auto repairs. A friend reports that he knows "where a crown—expertly done—is less than $100."

Significant numbers of Mexican and Asian residents add dimensions to the human geography of Imperial Beach.

Non-Mainstream Recreation (3 of 5 pts)

I.B. is the "only beach in Southern California where anyone can ride horses on the beach." Horses may be rented from the D-Bar-D Stables (619/428-2563). There is also a unique T-shaped fishing pier extending 1,200 feet out into the ocean. Fishing is free, with no license required. Residents say it's good for halibut and Florida bass.

The best fishing may soon diminish as an international conglomerate sets to inaugurate (at this writing) a new sewage plant that will divert the raw sewage that often escapes from Tijuana when the Mexican treatment plant breaks down. Prior to the new plant, the sewage drew sharks to the mouth of the trickling Tijuana River, closing the I.B. public beach on occasion. These "bon vivant" gourmet sharks were easy prey for waiting fishermen.

The Tijuana River National Estuarine Research Reserve, one of only 22 in the U.S., is the best remaining saltwater marsh wetland in Southern California, having survived for two reasons; the railroad veers inland before it gets to I.B., and the town has held sway against the developers.

A free visitors' center offers one-of-a-kind exhibits, including an interactive art genre called polage.

Using this technique, the artist, Austine Wood-Camarow, paints with polarized light. You can only see the work through a polarized lens. Colors and figures change when you rotate the polarizing filter, enabling a view of life cycles in their adaptive sequences.

Independent Politics (2 of 3 pts)

None of the salient features of I.B. would have survived without the town's independent voting habits, which have spared it from high-rise condos and hotels that extend along the rest of the Southern California coast, interrupted only by the San Onofre Nuclear Power Plant. You don't hear much about political affiliations because it's a one-issue town. The issue is land use. "It's not a party line situation," says Dottie.

The local weekly, *The Imperial Beach Times*, publishes editorials with titles such as "Reduce The Oligarchy," and applauds a City Councilmember's "decision to form a citizens' budget committee, a wonderful step backward, if you will, to a place in the past where it still was common belief that the American idea of self-government was a good one."

Public Hangouts (5 pts)

"Participatory" is not simply a buzzword for government. It extends into restaurants. The I.B. Forum, a barbecue place across from the beach, recognizes that many of its clients may excel at this particular cuisine art form, so if you choose, they'll sell you the meat and you may barbecue it as you wish.

The Pier Plaza, with its fountain and public restrooms, is a local gathering place and the site of many community events. International Blends Coffee Shop offers music on Friday nights. If you play classical or jazz, apply for a gig at 619/429-0340. There are also surfer hangouts, and of course, the beach itself is a place to be.

Mixed-Use Zoning (3 of 4 pts)

On the two main commercial corridors of this small city, residential units steadfastly remain. According to several residents we interviewed, the regional mall just outside of I.B. has failed to lure away business from ma and pa.

Pedestrian Friendly (4 points)

Walking, bicycling and skateboarding eclipse the automobile as preferred means of transportation. A trolley to San Diego allows pedestrians access to a big city without the need to drive; buses connect the trolley depot with I.B. neighborhoods. The trolley is located in Palm City, just across the I.B. line.

Upended Facilities (0 pts)

Imperial Beach has several projects that would earn it points in this category should they be approved by the regulators. We'll wait and see what happens to a vacant firehouse and what odd locale a theater group is ultimately going to refurbish.

Positive-Expectation Gambling (2 pts)

Del Mar Race Track, north of San Diego, holds an annual summer meet. A few miles to the south of I.B. in Tijuana, one can bet on simulcasts from virtually every track in the U.S., as well as on the dogs.

Freedom in the Bedroom (2 pts)

A few miles away, across the border, Tijuana has cleaned up its image with a cultural center and other outlets for the dynamic artistry that is so typical of

Mexican culture, without, however, repressing its tolerance for dionysian principles. "The Coco Club is an old-style Tijuana whorehouse, one of the last of its kind that once flourished in this city before officials went on a zealous image-changing binge in the mid-Sixties."

Meanwhile, the State of California has passed four laws banning various forms of discrimination based on sexual orientation.

Imperial Beach's geography makes it like a shy recluse forced to remain at a menacing party. On one side there are the developers, lusting to rape a beachline. On the other side, an army of unemployed, thirsting for jobs that most U.S. citizens would not dream of taking.

Imperial Beach just happens to be sandwiched between California's two greatest issues: development and immigration. While these two historical dramas play out, I.B. somehow manages to remain its own unpretentious self.

TOTAL POINTS: 30

JEROME, ARIZONA

When people with unfeasible livelihoods live in a town with unfeasible geography, the result is a place that defies all labels. Here is a town that should have died several times over, only to metamorphize into something else each time.

Once dubbed "the wickedest town in the west," with its saloons, gambling and houses of ill repute, its most recent death occured in 1953, when Phelps-Dodge Copper Mines shut down its mining operation.

Unconventional Regional Customs (3 of 6 pts)

But Jerome, located in high foothills halfway between Phoenix and the Grand Canyon, was restored to a functioning place by a rag-tag bunch of artists, 60s refugees, survivalists, musicians and instrument makers, who bought the run-down Victorian homes from old miners who wanted to retire in Phoenix.

According to John Villani, in *The 100 Best Small Art Towns in America*, "with the wide open spaces of Prescott National Forest nearby, some of Jerome's residents enjoy a certain illegal horticultural activity that every now and then causes the local law enforcement authorities to break out their rakes, hoes, and machetes."

Today, even business people and landowners in Jerome can be seen with "earrings and ponytails," and the non-conformism goes deep beneath the surface as well.

Alternative Economy (3 pts)

Not only have Jerome's residents chosen livelihoods that will not likely ever break into the mass market, but they have settled in a place off the main highway and up in the hills where buyers of their arts and crafts are less likely to happen by. But thanks to Jerome's Art Park and its various galleries, potential art buyers have "discovered" the place.

Evidently that is not enough. According to one local artist, "People come here looking for inexpensive deals, and as a result a lot of Jerome's artists go hungry each night."

Bizarre Geography (5 of 6 pts)

The *Rough Guide* writers believe that Jerome is "possibly the only American town situated like one of the hill towns in Italy or Spain." Having lived in Europe, I would have to agree.

In fact, its wooden buildings, as desribed by Pat Linnell in *Trailer Life*, "hang so precariously from the steep slopes that a slight breeze might send them plummeting into the Verde Valley." The author is not simply waxing poetic, since, at the turn of the century, the town jail did indeed tumble more than 200 feet after a mining explosion shook it loose from its moorings. The concrete-and-iron structure survived intact, and today can be seen below Hull Avenue where it came to rest.

Indeed, a number of structures from Jerome's past that just sit there. Within the living town, a ghost town still survives.

Today, the city's upper slope is connected to the lower one, 1,500 feet below, by a 30-degree incline. The view from the top of Jerome stretches out 50 miles through pristine air to Sedona's red-rock country, with the San Francisco Peaks in the background, highlighted by snow-covered Mingus Mountain.

While most American towns gradually trickle away at their outskirts, Jerome has an abrupt beginning and a sudden exit, with no tedious, neon or billboard outskirts.

Jerome's intestines are made up of eighty-eight miles of mining tunnels dug beneath and around the town of about 450 inhabitants.

Upended Facilities (1 of 3 pts)

What used to be the home of Jenny Bauters, Jerome's leading madam, is now the Copper Shop. One original bordello, with authentic decor, still turns on its red light, but now it is a decent restaurant aptly named The House of Joy.

A strange castlelike house was once a Mexican Methodist Church, "constructed in 1939 from scrap lumber, mine timbers and discarded dynamite boxes," called the Powderbox Church by the townies.

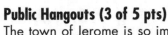

Public Hangouts (3 of 5 pts)

The town of Jerome is so impractical that it has very little commerce beyond its artistic endeavors, but for its places to hang out. So you can walk to a restaurant but you have to drive to the next town to the nearest grocery.

Along with The House of Joy, there is Paul & Jerry's Saloon on Main Street, a rowdy "time-warp trip into the wild West," according to Linnell.

The Spirit Room "does double duty," Villani explains, "as a dance hall and local hangout for the arts crowd."

Basic eats are served at the English Kitchen.

Absent from Jerome, national restaurant chains seem to know where they're not wanted.

Non-Mainstream Recreation & Entertainment (2 of 5 pts)

Less than 30 miles from Jerome, past Camp Verde and Route 17 is the clothing optional Verde Hot Springs, whose 104 degree springs make it a year-round "attraction," partly shielded from the cold winters by caves. As with most nudist retreats, finding this one is like going through a rat's maze. Check the route at a forest station. You'll know when you're close when you see "Get Nude" signs painted on the rocks.

Back in town, during the third weekend in May, Jerome's annual house tour allows visitors to enter a number of the renovated buildings, with local residents in vans shuttling you from place to place.

Independent Politics (1 of 3 pts)

The town has passed stiff zoning rules that favor patching up old buildings over constructing new ones, so there's a coherent architectural style. It does not have the look of a gentrified place, as residences are often in need of repair. (As a result of this policy, a three-bedroom home can still be had for $50,000, while in nearby Sedona, a similar-size but more mainstream home would cost you $200,000.) In the mid-sixties, houses could be had for $500.

Jerome's iconoclast nature has prevented it from becoming a mini-Santa Fe, which is good for the character of the town but bad for its economy.

As it stands today, Linnell is right when he affirms that "Jerome has to be Arizona's most unusual city." Given its weird location and the anarchism of many of its residents, it is likely to stay that way for a long time.

TOTAL POINTS: 18

KEY WEST, FLORIDA

After the bloody pirate wars of the early 1820s effectively rid the island of Key West of pirating, a new alternative economy emerged: wrecking and salvaging valuable cargo from numerous ships that ventured too close to the unmarked shallows and reefs off the coast. Key West became the wealthiest city per capita in the United States until a century later when the construction of lighthouses up and down the Keys effectively ended the lucrative "profession."

Unconventional Regional Customs (5 of 6 pts)

Key West is no less unique today. Its end-of-the-road geography has made it an ideal "last resort" for "dropouts and high rollers, runaways and roustabouts of all persuasions." According to Anne, interviewed by Thurston Clarke in a *Travel-Holiday* article, "Before moving here I didn't know anyone who'd been imprisoned. Now we have a lot of friends who've been in jail. They've become respected members of the business community, the Key West middle class."

Clarke refers to an acquaintance who entertained visitors with trained crabs. He was running for a seat on the city commission with the credo: "Fewer laws make fewer offenders."

Hemingway, a one-time resident, called it "...the last place to run to." Its eccentrics keep it separated in spirit from the Florida mainland.

One of their peculiar local customs is the nightly ritual at Mallory Square. A crowd gathers to observe the sunset, applauding at the moment when a brief green flash signals the final breath of sun.

Pedestrian Friendly (4 of 5 pts)

This ritual occurs in the setting of street musicians and entertainers (for example, a man juggling chain saws), along with food and craft vendors. Beyond Mallory Square, Key West is a feast for the eyes, best seen on foot. Buses, trolleys and a contour train further reduce the need to squeeze into a car.

The motley mix of people accompanies a bizarre concoction of architectural styles. From the Bahamas there are the overhanging eaves that cover extended porches. From New England comes the Greek Revival with sash windows and columns. From other nearby islands, there are louvered shutters that block out the hot sun while allowing the flow of cool breezes to come in. From New Orleans are African and Haitian-style cottages.

In most places, the "Old Town" is a small oasis within a larger sea of alienation, but in Key West, Old Town encompasses more than half the city, and everything is within walking distance. Just hang loose. Even the finest restaurants have no dress code.

 Cross-Cultural (5 pts)

The architecture is visual documentation of the cultural mix. Clarke relishes that Key West "accomodates Cubans, Conchs, blacks, gays, retirees, writers, fishermen, smugglers, sailors, and treasure hunters, enabling them to live in a harmony foreign to mainland cities."

The city is bilingual, thanks to the Cuban presence. Those born on the island, whose families sometimes go back seven generations, are called Conchs and represent a mix of Bahamian, Cuban and New England seafarers.

As one would expect, there is a wide variety of foods, with fish as a foundation. While upscale restaurants are abundant, there are also numerous family ethnic restaurants, most of them quite affordable, as well as lunch wagons on Duval Street.

Mixed-Use Zoning (4 pts)

Many of the ma-and-pa ethnic restaurants and groceries intermingle with residencial structures. The limited size of the island and its remoteness are its best protection against suburban sprawl and bland single-use areas.

Bizarre Geography (4 of 6 pts)

For this reason, Key West's geography is an active player in the life of the town, rather than a passive setting. There is a lack of variation and contrast in the climate, but Key West's weird location, at the extreme end of an archipelago, has kept away mainstream mainlanders and enticed eccentrics and runaways.

Its coral reef allows it to surpass other ocean front towns in the astonishing and unanticipated.

It is nearer to Havana, Cuba than to Miami, Florida.

Public Hangouts (5 pts)

The whole island is one big hangout. It all begins early, where the Cubans blend their potent espresso coffee with the art of conversation. Exuberant old men at a café table sound like a vocal jazz quartet.

The scene shifts to any number of outdoor eating spots, later drifting to Mallory Square. But festive sunset is merely a transition, not an ending.

There are waterside bistros for eating under the stars, streetside cafés, backyard patios, rooftop decks and more than one hundred watering holes, Jimmy Buffett's Margaritaville probably being the most famous.

Upended Facilities (1 of 3 pts)

Some of these hangouts as well as various offbeat shops are located in former Conch homes.

Non-Mainstream Recreation (2 of 5 pts)

When the sport of hanging out succeeds in slowing down the psychological clock, one can take a break and do something. Snorkelers can hunt through isolated coral patches, giant coral heads and deep drop-offs in search of wrecks originating as far back as the 17th century. A number of normal activities, such as boating, fishing and birdwatching, transcend the ordinary because of their connection to the area's unique geography.

To avoid anchoring on a reef, boaters can use mooring buoys, maintained by Reef Relief, an environmental education center. According Reef Relief, the living coral reef around Key West is the world's most biologically diverse marine ecosystem.

Alternative Economy (1 of 3 pts)

Thanks to the Mallory Square sunset ritual's groundrules, only home-made crafts may be sold during the festivities. Chains and multinationals can't compete with the local talent.

Independent Politics (2 of 3 pts)

Such customs are more likely to survive when the political system is not tied down to the two national parties. Local officials are all non-partisan and elections take place on the neighborhood level.

Freedom in the Bedroom (2 pts)

Of all cities and counties in Florida, Key West has the most sweeping set of ordinances barring discrimination based on sexual orientation.

Positive-Expectation Gambling (2 pts)

The FunKruz offers daily six-hour and evening cruises with losing propositions such as dice and spinning wheels, but also skill card games such as blackjack and various pokers, including Caribbean stud. Betting on sports events is also available.

With all the bizarre people and colorful settings, it is no surprise that the arts thrive in Key West. Theater involves local talent and easels are set up on Old Town streets, in abandoned movie houses and at backyard studios on unpaved lanes. Funky music can be heard in restaurants and bars.

Key West is a great place to be different or simply to express oneself, a hang-loose city where tolerance is the rule. According to Clarke, "only a small part of the island had been ruined by its own popularity."

TOTAL POINTS: 37

LILY DALE, NEW YORK

n the map, Lily Dale's small dot on a back road suggests a typical sleepy, western New York town. But this is the nation's unheralded capital of Spiritualism, a religion whose followers include mediums, clairvoyants and spiritual healers.

Unconventional Regional Customs (4 of 6 pts)

When I told one resident that I was visiting her town in order to eventually include it in a book about "unusual" places, she became defensive.

"We're just like anybody else," she shot back. "We have our post office and our cafeteria. We're *normal*. We just have our religion."

I imagine that truly different people often think that *they* are the normal ones. Since the town's by-laws prohibit non-spiritualists from owning property within the boundaries of Lily Dale, no resident is going to feel "different" here. But whether you believe in mediums and spiritual healing or not, let's accept the premise that the religion and culture of Spiritualism is on the fringe in relation to mainstream life in the USA.

Pedestrian Friendly (3 of 4 pts)

Subsequent chats and interviews proved to be a great deal friendlier than my first encounter, and that lady probably would have reacted more warmly had I not struck a bad chord. Since mediums are often ridiculed in the mainstream culture, I imagine she had a right to become touchy when she found out I was researching her town.

Anyway, one of the reasons why Lily Dale is an amicable place is its layout. Wooded streets and paths wind intimately about, from one old wood frame house to another, in an asymmetrical layout that invites one to take a stroll. Since each individual property is minimal when compared to the common grounds, the village's compactness also encourages going about one's business or pleasure on foot. The streets are too narrow for a car to pick up velocity, and some of them are topped with loose gravel, slowing down motor vehicles yet more.

Unfortunately, there is no grocery store within the village; thus, residents must go a mile and a half to Cassadaga for food, unless of course they take all their meals in the cafeteria.

Other features that can be reached on foot make up for that minor inconvenience. Nature trails, alluring Cassadaga Lake with its recreational facilities, the bandstand and gazebo, the picnic shelter, the assembly hall, the cafeteria and Inspiration Stump are all too near to use a car. Each structure has its history. For example, the Lily Dale Community Club was formerly an 1880 one-room school house.

Mixed-Use Zoning (3 of 4 pts)

There is no zoning in town. In fact, commercial, residential and recreational sites are all found in buildings that pass for houses. The few shops are as unassuming as a neighborhood garage sale. Most of the books and gifts being sold awaken one's curiosity in one way or another, but there are other items of dubious value, such as the "worry stone," made of Mexican onyx, used to "rub your troubles away" and selling for a mere 59 cents.

While one could argue that the absence of higher forms of commerce is refreshing, the zoning mix is incomplete without vital places such as a grocery or hardware store.

Alternative Economy (2 of 3 pts)

Apparently, most residents survive on activities related to Spiritualism, including seminars and various sessions covering spiritual healing, clairvoyance and "readings." I was not able to ascertain how much individuals can earn on the side with private gigs, but services rendered to groups are of minimal charge and most often free once the visitor has paid the modest gate fee, which is charged only from late June through early September.

Not anyone can arrive and set up a placard. One's mediumship must be certified by the local board.

Public Hangouts (2 of 5 pts)

Once inside the village gate, the whole place has the feel of an extended hangout. From cafeteria to lake beach to café, people are gathered in conversation. However, since there is so much purpose and structure in the town, the aimlessness that characterizes the best of hangouts will be missing.

Visitors may choose between two truly quaint, modestly-priced hotels, one originating in the 1880s. Alternative housing includes pitching a tent on the campgrounds or staying at one of several private guest homes.

The $5 gate fee, summers only, covers parking, auditorium lecture/clairvoyance, outdoor message services, the healing temple, the library (with the world's largest collection of spiritualist books) and the museum.

Visitors are advised that mediumship differs from fortune telling and that clients should enter readings with a flexible mind. They are also told that spiritual healing is not a substitute for modern medicine. You won't find any Jimmy Swaggart look-alikes in Lily Dale.

Particularly impressive was the tasty food and friendly service at the village's greasy spoon cafeteria, housed in an old two story wood structure with a wrap-around screen-enclosed porch. I wasn't there long enough to get tired of the moderately priced cafeteria food, but for variety, one can scoot into Cassadaga for dinner at Grandma's Family Kitchen.

For information on the extensive array of events and seminars, both in season and off, phone 716/595-8721.

TOTAL POINTS: 14

LOPEZ ISLAND AND NORTH PUGET SOUND REGION, WASHINGTON

How about a place with no traffic lights, where "hitchhiking is considered safe and easy...you start walking from the ferry landing, somebody will probably offer you a ride without seeing any thumbs."

This is a place where "the wave" was invented. It may sound corny but everyone waves to each other, perhaps because they are all co-conspirators in voluntary anachronism.

Unconventional Regional Customs (2 of 6 pts)

Lopez Island is one of the four largest San Juan Islands in Puget Sound, sometimes referred to as "Slowpez" by its inhabitants, for whom a "Lopezotomy" is what happens to one's brain after spending time on the Island.

Lopez does not resort to a self-conscious or mannered routine for perpetuating the past. While the Pennsylvania Dutch, for example, are visibly in touch with the past, economically they are moving into the commercial mainstream. Lopez, on the other hand, maintains a medieval economy.

Alternative Economy (2 of 3 pts)

Unlike most businessmen, Lopez entrepreneurs shun expansion. Larry Vetter makes his living stirring up hot mustards and barbecue sauces, marketing them at the San Juan Islands ma-and-pa stores and open-air markets. He didn't list his business in the phone book because the ad costs fifty bucks. Then there's Jim Poth, who calls himself a countryside guide and operates van and bicycle tours.

The small, family-run Glencorra Farm specializes in sheep's milk cheese, relatively undiscovered in the USA, and visitors can have a free taste. Lopez's abandoned orchards are being taken over by microfarmers, in a total turnaround from the current agricultural trend.

"We don't care to get so big that we have to cater to stores," says one local farmer.

Lopez even has the Lopez Island Vineyards, from which you can order Chardonnay and Cabernet Sauvignon by mail (206/468-3644). Other Lopez products may be ordered by direct mail, including salmon jams and sauces.

Meanwhile, eighteen Lopez artists operate Gallery Chimera, a co-op in the center of the tiny village.

Bizarre Geography (3 of 6 pts)

Isolated like No-Roads-Lead-To-Nome, Alaska, Lopez is without a bridge connecting it to the mainland. One can suspect that the isolation of places reached only by ferry nurtures a unique culture. For example, cyclists here find themselves in control of the transportation system, bestowed with a 38-mile bike loop and three bicycle stores to get set up.

With 60 populated islands in the San Juans alone, and various places of interest on North Puget Sound's mainland coast, this is an ideal region to hop from place to place. Thanks to the region's mottled geography, most of these places have maintained their own unique character.

In particular, LA Conner, less than an hour southeast of Lopez Island, on the mainland, holds on to much of what was originally constructed prior to the arrival of the railroads in the late 1880s. A city ordinance requires new buildings to have a turn-of-the-century architecture, and residents are willing to pay the added expense in order to preserve what they've got.

LA Conner is located on the Swinomish Channel. Historically, the town has been a haven for non-conformists (Wobblies, WWII COs, McCarthy-era escapees, beatniks, hippies and bikers). Today it's somewhat of an artists' colony, with waterfront businesses built on pilings. Unlike most "middleman" tourist shopping traps, LA Conner's bazaar sells a large percentage of locally produced products, including the edible art at the Calico Cupboard.

"There are lots of craftsmen left over from the hippie days," one LA Conner resident explained.

Although the Native American Swinomish community across the channel (over the Rainbow Bridge) maintains its separate culture, one resident explained that there's lots of interaction between the communities in the realm of sports and commerce.

The ocean and air currents of the Pacific Northwest give the Puget Sound area a very benign climate compared to places on similar lattitudes in the midwest and east.

Most of the San Juan Islands receive only half the rainfall of nearby Seattle, thanks to being in the rainshadow of the Olympic Mountains.

Pedestrian Friendly (1 of 4 pts)

Lopez Island is too large to do all one's business on foot, yet the village itself is too small for a long walk. But with hitchhiking so easy, walkers are never out of place. In places where the bicycle culture dominates, the pedestrian is not overwhelmed by the automobile culture. Hiking and beachcombing are further incentives to travel in an upright position.

(Meanwhile, LA Conner's street life offers a funkier alternative to pastoral Lopez.)

Upended Facilities (1 of 3 points)

The public library looks like an old red schoolhouse, but claims to have the highest rate of book use in the state. At the ferry landing, is Faeries Landing, a trailer converted into a restaurant.

Non-Mainstream Recreation (2 of 5 pts)

Kayaking by day or by moonlight in Lopez's myriad of bays and coves is facilitated by Lopez Bicycle Works. As an alternative to whale watching, there is sea lion watching at Shark Reef.

Public Hangouts (1 of 5 pts)

Lopez has a public hangout, too. The outdoor wooden tables at Holly B's Bakery are a favorite spot for locals and tourists alike, "a perfect place to slip into Lopez time." (In LA Conner, the Café Pojante espresso bar in the loft above Skagit Bay Books is a spirited town gathering place.)

Ironically, Lopez Island was saved from the dominant economic culture when its large fruit orchards were eclipsed by the Yakima Valley with the construction of the Grand Coulee Dam. Meanwhile,

LA Conner can fight off becoming young thanks to vital infusions of money from Seattle, since new buildings with old craftsmanship are not cheap.

The region of North Puget Sound thrives with an eclectic array of nooks and crannies, with Lopez Island and LA Conner as worthy focal points.

TOTAL POINTS: 12

LOVE CANAL, NEW YORK

Would you buy a house in proximity to an ominous looking "containment area deemed to be non-habitable," a vast, flattened dome covered over with grass and blocked off with a chain-link fence. Within the fenced-off area are black gondolas with who knows what sludge piled inside.

Would it appeal to you to relocate near a storage site that contains 22,000 tons of toxic wastes? And what about the fact that the 239 houses immediately surrounding the dump had been demolished, or that a multitude of other houses remain boarded up along eerily vacated streets?

Would the grafitti on an abandoned church dissuade you?... LEAD AND MERCURY HERE. Or the fact that many of the refurbished homes for sale at bargain rates are right next to abandoned, weathered houses that may never again be resuscitated!

How about eerie 100th Street, with all of its houses boarded up, overrun now with the macabre beauty of lush foliage!

Actually, there were two evacuations of the original Love Canal. The first one, in 1978, was widely considered necessary. The need for the second evacuation, however, is still controversial among scientists.

With evidence of various strange ailments plaguing the residents who lived near the dioxin-laden creeks, a federal judge found Hooker Chemical, alias Occidental Chemical, liable for handling wastes in a way that would eventually result in chemical seepage. Surely the company did not change its name to avoid the embarrassment of its women employees going to work with jackets labeled "Hooker." Area residents believe the name change resulted strictly because of Hooker's having shamelessly dumped its sizzling waste for years into the river.

Today, as you drive through the industrial area between Love Canal and Niagara Falls, you'll see a sign above the street at the new Hooker: SAFETY—IT'S A FAMILY CONCERN—OXYCHEM.

Unconventional Regional Customs (3 of 6 points)

If the first chapter of the Love Canal drama was full of pathos and fury, the second chapter is one of irony and caricature. Sixty households stayed behind in the boarded-up neighborhoods. "Ironically," writes Michael H. Brown in *The Atlantic*, "the depopulation has turned the area into a wild-life refuge." Florence Best, one of the stayers, enjoys bird watching and says, "the whole world's polluted, no matter where you go."

Strange rashes and warts have diminished or disappeared for some of the luckier victims since they moved away. Meanwhile, a new crop of settlers is currently moving into the four of seven Love Canal areas that are now considered "habitable" by the EPA.

Hooker Chemical was not the only one to change its name because of the big mess. The Love Canal Area Revitalization Agency is making a heroic effort to condition folks to call the area Black Creek Village.

A further irony in this ongoing story is the fact that, at a time when real estate prices across the nation were plummeting, Love Canal is one of the few places where prices have been appreciating. Strange that the real estate agents don't take advantage of this with ads about the "mercurial rise in sales."

Sales thus far are no doubt partly triggered by the discounts offered to buyers, initially 20 percent, later reduced to 15 percent and scheduled to be further reduced to 10 percent at some point.

Over 60 percent of the renovated homes have been occupied. We interviewed a representative of the Revitalization Agency, who proudly explained that you can get a house for fifty thousand in an all-new neighborhood that doesn't have the barrenness of new subdivisions since there are 40-year-old trees.

Buyers include young, first-home purchasers, extended families, firemen, policemen, single women, single men, gay couples and lesbian couples. They all have one weird thing in common; they are willing to take a chance on the most devastated toxic waste site in recent history, in order to save a few bucks.

This writer recently sold a home at a loss. If the "state-of-the-art" containment system is indeed effective, Love Canal residents will be able to tell me that I'm the one who made a dumb investment, not them.

Still, one Buffalo resident, shaking his head and grimacing, told me he wouldn't live in Love Canal if you gave him the house for free. Some environmental scientists still consider the place "a ticking time bomb."

Bizarre Geography (3 of 6 pts)

The fact that parts of the non-habitable areas will eventually become parks and that wildlife flourishes precisely where environmental purists saw a great disaster is bizarre enough. But Love Canal has another geographic asset. It is only five minutes from Niagara Falls. No matter how many times I visit the Falls, the wonderment never diminishes. Between Love Canal and Niagara Falls are parks where one can follow the rapids just before they reach the falls.

Cross-Cultural (2 of 5 pts)

The final demographic description of the new Love Canal remains to be seen, but meanwhile, its proximity with Ontario, Canada offers a certain degree of cultural variety. From the looks of things as I went through the neighborhood street by street, there is an exemplary ethnic mix developing in the new Love Canal.

Non-Mainstream Entertainment (1 of 5 pts)

For some time, tour buses were going through Love Canal. Eventually, it will either become a monument to man-made disaster or a testimony to how things can be turned around. According to new homeowner Tammy Bunce, the tourists "were staring at us in our yards like we were going to glow."

Sam Giarrizzo, who never left his original Love Canal house, cracks jokes about how he glows. But is anyone of the stayers joking about their kids glowing in the dark?

Were it not for the catastrophe, certain streets of Love Canal would be looking like any other dull suburban neighborhood. But with monumental chain fences, state-of-the-art containment areas and residents who proudly defy common wisdom, this neighborhood will remain unique for quite some time, if not forever.

Says one former Niagara Falls resident whose nephew once came back from playing barefoot in Love Canal with burns on his feet:

"Creeks run underneath the containment area. Sooner or later, erosion will have to take place."

Positive-Expectation Gambling (2 pts)

One might argue that every Love Canal resident is a gambler by nature, betting on the wisdom of EPA analysts. But if the thrill wears off from that gamble, there is a harness race track in nearby Buffalo, and thoroughbreds who run at Fort Erie, Ontario, a ten-minute drive away.

TOTAL POINTS: 11

MADAWASKA, MAINE

Want to go back in time, to real wilderness, untransformed by fast food corporations, freeways and current events? When was the last time that a news item from Maine made the Nightly News?

Can't find any "places rated" book that goes north of Bangor and Maine survives without a professional sports franchise.

Cross-Cultural (3 of 5 pts)

Madawaska is four hours north of Bangor but only three hours south of Quebec City. The residents are descendants of Acadian French, Micmac and Maliseet Indians, and Swedish settlers. They speak English and/or French.

If you could turn the Mardi Gras inside out, you'd come up with June 28 Acadian Day, a celebration of the local cultural roots. These are the original Cajuns, those French-speaking Acadians who were not forcibly removed from Maine-Canada to be transported to Louisiana and other unlikely spots in the hemisphere. In fact, the Acadian settlement predated Jamestown!

Acadian Day includes food, dance, arts and crafts, and the Acadian Mass. Recently, this Festival has been a medium for reuniting Madawaska Acadians with their Cajun brothers and sisters. Cajun bands come to perform and there are bizarre family reunions: same family but radically different cultures.

Another regional cultural dimension involves the old logging tradition. Ten miles south, in Ashland, you can attend a lumberjack competition in early July. Exploring the backwoods, one travels over unpaved lumber roads leading to places like Horse Race Rapids and Caribou.

Everyone has heard of Route 1, but not many have traced it to its source near the Canadian border. Route 1 ends (or begins) in the town of Fort Kent, not far from Madawaska.

Bizarre Geography (3 of 6 pts)

The Madawaska region is the northern-most part of mainland USA, virtually ignored by the rest of this nation. Fort Kent is the gateway to the vast Aroostook wilderness. Visitors will need a permit to use the private logging roads.

There are more than 2,000 lakes, streams and ponds, in a region surrounded on 3 sides by Canada.

Unconventional Regional Customs (3 of 6 pts)

In nearby Houlton, historic barracks are a reminder of the world's most unsung "unconventional" war, the

Bloodless Aroostook War, settled by treaty before the first shot was fired.

This is potato country. In Fairfield, one can attend or participate in mashed potato wrestling. More significant, the Aroostook potato harvest is nationally unique; it is the only area in USA where children are excused from school to help harvest: potato digging with backdrop of splendid fall foliage.

Non-Mainstream Recreation (2 of 5 pts)

Non-traditional activities include ice fishing, snowshoe exploring, the Fort Kent Mardi Gras (February), the Maine Dirigo 250 Dog Sled Race from Houlton to Fort Kent, the region's version of Alaska's Iditarod (February), the Aroostook River Raft Race, from Caribou to Fort Fairfield (July), and mashed potato wrestling.

Above all, though, the Madawaska region is a nation to itself which covers territory on both sides of the Maine/French Canadian border. "Though we have lost our lovely Acadia," write the festival sponsors, "never will we forget her. We will continue to speak her language, sing her songs, and forever hold dear her traditions; for the spirit of those first Acadians lives on in us, her descendants."

TOTAL POINTS: 11

MISSION DISTRICT, SAN FRANCISCO, CALIFORNIA

Nobody doubts that San Francisco is a stimulating, quirky, city. But today, a prevalent feature of certain districts in this city is blatant nostalgia, so the question is: what have you done lately? Furthermore, with hypergentrification, how many of us would be priced out of the neighborhood?

Yet, there are signs that this city will forever generate countercultural movements. One recent San Francisco cultural phenomenon coincides with a fundamental idea of this book, that the dominance of the automobile diminishes the quality of life, isolates people from each other, creates a geography of sensory deprivation, and turns us into unexercised half torsos.

Critical Mass is an extraordinary monthly happening in which bicycles clog city streets during rush hours. The term "critical mass" was used by urban cyclists in China, who needed to gather in large numbers in order to safely cross busy intersections.

Organized by the San Francisco Bike Coalition and the Auto-Free Bay Area Coalition, Critical Mass has been spreading to other cities. Participants protest that city life deteriorates when there is the need to move large numbers of cars through small spaces.

Critical Mass is one of various grass roots movements remaining as a rich undercurrent of San Francisco's character. And there are still pockets within the city where the less affluent can survive and thrive. One of these places is The Mission District.

Predominantly Hispanic (Mexican and Central American), an influx of young cutting-edge artists has given the neighborhood a distinct "rive gauche" character.

Pedestrian Friendly (4 pts)

The Mission has the largest concentration of city murals, many of them with Hispanic themes in the tradition of the great Mexican muralist, Diego Rivera. Within an area of 8 blooks in the southwest part of The Mission, you can see more than 60 murals.

The neighborhood gets its name from "Misión Dolores," San Francisco's oldest building, which has survived all the great earthquakes and fires of modern Bay Area history. Its ceiling, in a traditional Native American design, was painted by the Costanoan Indians.

Every block offers a new twist to incite the senses, from bright, renovated Victorian homes on streets around Hill and Liberty, to mango and ice cream stands, specialty book stores, and lots of people on the streets and in the parks.

Gordon, a young punk music fan, puts it this way:

"The neighborhood is extremely oriented to the pedestrian. Most people I know don't even have cars."

Two BART (SF subway) stops, on Mission at 16th and 24th provide the transportation ingredient that virtually eliminates the need to drive.

Alternative Economy (3 pts)

Life on the street is typically enhanced when there are bottom-up enterprises. The Mission has thrift stores, vendors with push-carts selling street food and produce, and relatively inexpensive alternative theater.

Marcus, who lives and works in the neighborhood, likes the fact that The Mission "is shot through with ma-and-pa stores."

There is a down side, Gordon says. "Although lots of street people have regular spaces where they sell things, there have been crackdowns against these people, and against the group Food Not Bombs, for regularly distributing free food to The Mission's homeless residents," without a license.

Public Hangouts (5 pts)

With murals, help for homeless residents, ma-and-pa stores and outdoor vendors, The Mission is a very public place.

"There are tons of coffee shops around Valencia and 16th Street," says Marcus with civic pride, "and lots of regulars hang out in Dolores Park, dog walkers and neighborhood soccer players, for example."

An increasing number of bars, some with music and poetry, dance spaces, and shops where browsers chat without being hassled, make The Mission "the place" to hang out.

Epicenter is one of these shops, with a large collection of new and used punk-rock albums and independent "zines."

People can hang out at the Epicenter's political and zine library without feeling obligated to make a purchase; this can unpredictably transmute into a spontaneous gathering place with a party atmosphere while other times it remains mellow.

Some of the old hangouts have been dying because of gentrification, adds Gordon, but Marcus responds that "it would take an awful lot of gentrification to destroy this place and there are various independent neighborhood groups that are addressing the problem."

Independent Politics (2 of 3 pts)

Gordon doesn't seem encouraged by the political scene, but affirms that "people keep trying." The Food Not Bombs members get carted off to jail from time to time but they always come back. More tempered neighborhood groups are dedicated to local and global issues, and the San Francisco spirit of creative contrarianism that engendered Critical Mass is certainly thriving.

Cross-Cultural (3 of 5 pts)

Gordon explains that "the white, hip subculture doesn't necessarily mix that well with other groups," but he labels the neighborhood "somewhat cross-cultural."

Marcus is more optimistic in this respect. "The neighborhood sponsors several major events to bring the diverse cultures together," including "Carnaval" San Francisco, on Memorial Day, a type of Mardi Gras event that celebrates carnival traditions around the world.

The Cesar Chavez trilingual school (English, Spanish and Amercian Sign Language), with its murals by children and adults, is one of various multicultural symbols in the community.

Upended Facilities (1 of 3 pts)

Clearly, in the Mission District, the dictionary definition of "wall" needs to be changed to "canvas." The Mexican mural painters have reincarnated.

Non-Mainstream Entertainment (4 of 5 pts)

The multicultural composition of the nighborhood is the foundation of many of its attractions. The Precita Eyes Mural Arts Center's Saturday tours include a how-to-do-your-own-mural slide show. The adobe Misión Dolores is San Francisco's answer to Europe's aged structures, where one is seduced back in time through the senses.

The "Carnaval," an abundance of inexpensive alternative theater, poetry readings, outdoor art, barroom music and funky bookstores are just a few of the neighborhood's offerings. Just being there is entertainment.

(Across town, Baker Beach, beneath the Presidio, with the Golden Gate Bridge in view, is a clothing optional beach; a ferry will take you to Angel Island, in the Bay, where the amicable wildlife includes nudist hikers.)

Unconventional Regional Customs (5 of 6 pts)

While one might call The Mission an "alternative" place, it is better labeled a neighborhood of alternatives. A variety of cultural and philosophical avenues lead in diverse directions.

The New College, on Valencia Street, is a center of alternative education that offers a degree in poetics and has innovative programs on art and activism, while housing a women's resource center.

Good Vibrations, also on Valencia, is a vibrator and sex-toy store "that's so respectable of the sacred act, you could almost bring your mom there."

Club Commotion, run by a collective, offers an eclectic array of alternative music, including punk and rap, while at Epicenter, anarchists feel at home.

"A different person," Gordon explains, "will feel more comfortable in this neighborhood than in other places."

Marcus adds that much of what we would label unconventional customs are behind the scenes and may not be apparent, but there are lots of unconventional people in The Mission.

Bizarre Geography (5 of 6 pts)

As an interior San Francisco neighborhood, the Mission District is shielded from the extremes of the Bay and is therefore unplagued by fog. While locals might complain about the relatively cool summers and sometimes raw winters, in reality, the San Francisco Bay Area offers the least antagonistic climate in the United States; thanks to a confluence of ocean currents, it is one of the very few places in the USA that never gets too cold nor too hot.

The people can live with the scare of an occasional thirty-second earth shaker, knowing that ice storms and blizzards unknown to this region are a much greater cause of death and suffering.

The city's drastic and sometimes preposterous geography of ups and downs creates a variety of nooks and crannies, providing psychic relief from the flatness of modern uniformity.

Mixed-Use Zoning (4 pts)

As far as man-made geography is concerned, residence and commerce are not segregated into dull, one-dimensional zones, especially along the 24th Street corridor.

Positive-Expectation Gambling (2 pts)

Golden Gate Fields race track is just across the Bay in Albany, and Bay Meadows, the other local track, is not far to the south. There is quality racing at both plants, which alternate meets. A publication called *Today's Racing Digest* will give you an extra edge in the information-age contest of the mind that characterizes smart horse investing.

Freedom of the Bedroom (2 pts)

San Francisco's "Gay Mecca," The Castro, is just to the west of The Mission. The heterosexual revolution of the sixties also began in this city. As could be guessed, San Francisco has passed the most comprehensive set of laws banning discrimination based on sexual preference.

Several travel books have noted that the Mission District does not qualify as the safest place in the USA, but the residents I interviewed did not express any serious concern.

Within a high-rent city, The Mission still offers folks with a modest income an affordable place to rent. The neighborhood's Mexican restaurants are the authentic family "bistros" of San Francisco, dishing up an affordable and tasty alternative to the city's more upscale cuisine.

The Mission District is the largest of several zones within San Francisco that carry on the city's funky traditions without pricing out whole sectors of society.

TOTAL POINTS: 40

NEW ORLEANS, LOUISIANA

There was never any question that New Orleans is a funky place. But with this city, the threat of "cliché" gets in the way of an objective description. With the help of a few hard-core New Orleans residents, especially the perceptive Gary McMillan (G.M.), we will do our best to break through the cliché barrier.

(Parentheses will denote my comments. Otherwise, our sources will do the talking.)

Unconventional Regional Customs (6 pts)

G.M.: So much of what is unique about New Orleans flows out of Mardi Gras. A two-week carnival of masking, acting out inhibitions, letting go, releasing original nature.

The reason I don't go crazy during the year is that I don't live in Omaha, and I can allow myself to go crazy, get dirty, act silly, take off the mask, once a year at Carnival. My theory is that Mardi Gras also works its healing magic, consciously or unconsciously, on thousands of other people...

Jazz Funerals: slow moving street musicians going down Claiborne Avenue, playing slow, dark, heavy funeral dirges that suddenly erupt into wild brass band dancing and "second-lining" on the way to the graveyard. (Second-lining is a music of African American origin that overhauls well-known musical themes. It is heard in day-long street celebrations that set entire neighborhoods dancing. The Dirty Dozen and ReBirth Brass Bands are the best-known practitioners of this music.)

G.M.: When older musicians die here, they take you out with the tune called "Didn't He Ramble."

Lagniappe is a little something extra, something for nothing. A little treat of kindness or giving. You can still go to the bakery and ask for a dozen rolls and get thirteen. You just got lagniappe. Not as prevalent as it used to be, you still bump into lagniappe in some of the small neighborhood stores.

Red beans and rice on Monday, the poor-man's dish. You get ham hocks, a piece of smoked sausage, red beans, rice, a loaf of French bread. This is a real deal. Every Monday like clockwork.

Voodoo shops where you can buy "lucky dust" and "money oil," and a highly superstitious population. Middle-aged women and older, for example, tell you that "nakedness draws lightening." Put your shirt on or don't walk around barefoot when there is thunder and lightening. My favorite superstition, however, is something called "The Holy Ghost." This is a theory that events happen in sequences of three. Father, Son and Holy Ghost.

Politics? Think of banana republic when you think of New Orleans. In an election for Governor, the choices were David Duke and Edwin Edwards. It gets worse at the local level. Corruption, bribes, indictments are part and parcel of the political fabric. On one occasion, Louie Roussell, horse and casino owner, handed out envelopes of cash on the floor of the state senate. Campaign contributions. Our greedy lawmakers were lined up like grocery clerks in a questionable spectacle that would have raised the eyebrows of concerned citizens anywhere but Louisiana. The last real independent candidate was probably Jim Garrison. He was an honest rogue not likely to be duplicated in the coming century.

Trends: New Orleans is repellent for things that are fashionable, as opposed to places like California, where the half-life of a fad might last 45 minutes.

Lack of pretense: more than any other single reason that I choose to live in New Orleans is the unpretentiousness of the people. There is a distinct lack of self-absorbed, self-righteous people here. It shows up as a kind of irreverence for all things too serious and dignified. Who really cares? I'm convinced that this lack of pretense flows out of the spirit of Mardi Gras and is manifested on a daily basis with behaviors that drive Type A perfectionists up, and off, the wall.

Bizarre Geography (1 of 6 pts)

G.M.: Mark Twain lived here for some time and once had words on the strangeness of the local climate: "If you find you don't like the weather in New Orleans just wait five minutes." He was probably talking about the huge thunderstorms that can develop quickly off the Gulf and pass over the city, dropping more rain in two hours than Southern Califonria gets in an entire year.

My ambition is to play golf in a hurricane. I have almost fulfilled this dream on two occasions but my playing partner opted for higher ground both times. No guts, no glory.

Cross-Cultural (4 of 5 pts)

G.M.: I have a layman's theory. It goes like this...money, fame, wealth and power are insidious insulators. Money insulates people from people. The more you have, the more separated you become. If New Orleans is anything, it is a city of poor folks. Fewer barriers exist here because there is less wealth. Sure there are social barriers but for the most part everybody hangs out together.

In the food, in the language, in the colors and architecture, in the music...the French, the Spanish, the Black Creole Caribbean influences are all around us.

It seems that most cultures and traditions are represented in some fashion, and mostly without separation and barriers. There is no "Chinatown" or "Little Italy" but these ethnic groups can be found spread throughout the city. There is a distinct neighborhood called the "Irish Channel" but there are as many Cubans and Hondurans there as descendants from the Emerald Isle.

Food? My God! With a little planning you could eat at a restaurant that reflects a unique culture each day of the month.

Vietnamese Village is the only exception to this cross-cultural profile. The Vietnamese have located mostly in New Orleans East, along a large bayou and nearby marsh. I go there on Saturday mornings to buy fish and fresh vegetables. There is a kind of illegal market, very open and very pleasurable but without taxes and licenses and health inspectors. It's Saigon. A wild scene that few white men will ever witness or even imagine that it exists. Live chickens, rabbits and turtles are sold on the roadside. Inside a housing compound, tables and floormats with herbs, fruits, vegetables. Prices are negotiable. I pay 50 cents for a bag of fresh ginger that would cost me five dollars at supermarkets.

(Gary's cross-cultural vision is tempered by Beth and her minister father, Bob, both from New Orleans.)

Beth: In some ways, Gary is right. You'd be hard-pressed to find a white person in New Orleans who doesn't have a black friend. You don't have the segregation of northern cities; it's more like a checkerboard, a few blocks black, a few blocks white. But there's an enormous racial complexity, and yes, tension in New Orleans. The harmony that exists in the arts community doesn't translate into the commercial or professional sector.

Bob: There's no open conflict or sparring between groups, and you have the open-minded French Quarter, where there's no distinction between groups. But there is a strong underlying prejudice. Most whites are somewhat resentful that blacks have "taken over the city." Yet, there's still a lot of openness and mixing; the French element has always been that way.

A large number of whites have moved out of the city and are now in Jefferson Parrish, where David Duke has a following.

(New Orleans historian Joe Logsdon sums up the cultural contradictions. For him, what defines New Orleans is that it has given birth to an indigenous culture. "Boston will always have a Puritan influence. Virginia will always have that feeling of gentry. Minneapolis will always feel Scandinavian. Santa Fe will always feel Hispanic." But since New Orleans doesn't have reference in a single Old World Culture, it will "always feel Creole."

Logsdon adds that the island-like quality of New Orleans forced people to commingle. "And when people commingle, cultures develop." No one ethnic group has ever dominated New Orleans historically.

But "culture is a fragile thing." The threats are coming from new forms of segregation and suburbanization. "People can escape New Orleans into self-enclosed communities. When you close your doors to your neighbors and wall them off from you, you lose the fertile ground for the creation of culture.")

Alternative Economy (3 pts)

G.M. Vietnamese Village is but one illustration of New Orleans' open economy.

I first came here in August of 1966. I had $18 in my pocket. It was hot. After walking around for awhile, I stumbled into a barroom where I had heard Dizzy Gillespie, Coltrane and Miles Davis on the juke-box. The name of the joint was Big Time Crip's.

It was obvious that I was a stranger. Not many white boys wander into a black uptown ghetto with a duffel bag and spend the afternoon listening to jazz classics on the jukebox. After awhile, the owner came over to my table and checked me out. As soon as he felt reassured that I was not an undercover cop, he said, "Son, if you stick around I'll keep the cheat off you. Don't worry about a thing. If you can't make it in New Orleans, you can't make it anywhere. This is Big Easy, Louisiana."

To put it mildly, there is no lack of alternative solutions to mainstream concepts of work in New Orleans. The French Market is blocks and blocks of produce stands, fruits and vegetables in season, organically-grown or otherwise, a farmer's market, a wholesale and retail bazaar; it opens early and goes all day.

The used goods market is vibrant in New Orleans, primarily strung out along Magazine Street.

I know a few guys who survive salvaging lost golf balls out of ditches, bayous, lakes and ponds. Minimum overhead required in this profession: a pair of swimming trunks and a bucket makes you an instant entrepreneur.

A good friend makes quite a good living landscaping people's homes. Gardening, grass cutting...from May through August you can virtually watch the grass grow; the tropics are a plant paradise.

(Gwen Sheperd, "the pie lady," makes $300 a week in profit although she spends six days a week baking and sells over 250 pies Wednesdays and Fridays, in the central business district.

A nun, Sister Roddy, labeled "Sister Act," sells her watercolors in the French Quarter...Musicians sitting in Royal Street, playing for change, youngsters tap-dancing, Jackson Square clowns making balloon animals for children.)

G.M.: There is a growing interest in alternative medicine. A person with the proper amounts of passion and technical knowledge can master an ancient art and make money at the same time.

I make New Orleans the perfect habitat for a writer. It's like living in an incubator. Faulkner wrote his first novel while living in the French Quarter. Read *A Walk On the Wild Side* by Nelson Algren and that will tell you everything.

Public Hangouts (5 pts)

G.M.: There is an abundance of public hangouts, outdoors and indoors, the lakefront, City Park, the river levee, Audubon Park (where I practice Tai Chi), lots of good Chi, the St. Charles Street Car, an ambling kind of hangout for people to meet people, the same feeling as the San Francisco trolleys except that it lasts longer...from Canal Street to the university section, and the conductors are not as rude. (And of course, the bars, many of the neighborhood ones with their regulars.)

Pedestrian Friendly (4 pts)

G.M.: We're talking about the New Orleans that nobody knows about, where every neighborhood has one or two barrooms, a seafood restaurant, a sandwich shop, a little bakery, a bar-b-que joint.

After mowing the front yard, it is not unusual for me to walk two blocks over to Henry's House and have a cold beer, or my son will bike up to Cast-Net Restaurant and bring back a couple of oyster po-boy sandwiches. Most everything is close like that. Not many people choose to live without a car these days, but you could pull it off in New Orleans.

I take the bus back and forth to work quite often. A very good and inexpensive public transport system.

The central business district, the French Quarter, and the riverfront are not a huge urban sprawl: rather compressed and walkable for the visitor who can learn to become less impetuous.

Mixed-Use Zoning (4 pts)

G.M.: Bars, restaurants, bakeries, all this blends into the neighborhood. This is certainly not a city of condominiums. There are a few but the concept does not agree with the lifestyles of the peasant population.

What we call "shot-gun" doubles is the standard abode for mixing living with your own business. One building with two doors. It can be like a double apartment, or it can accommodate you and your family on one side and your record store, your day care, your leather goods, your ceramic shop or your massage parlor on the other.

Upended Facilities (3 pts)

G.M.: The 1984 World's Fair was a fiscal fiasco, but it did leave us with a rejuvenated, cleaned-up warehouse district that was turned into one of the neatest pockets of the city. Century-old brick warehouses stretched along the riverfront, housing a cluster of interesting new restaurants, night clubs, coffee houses, offices and art galleries.

A policy of the new Mayor to renovate abandoned property into single residential homes appears to have serious intent.

Non-Mainstream Entertainment and Recreation (5 pts)

G.M.: Sitting on the seawall with three pounds of boiled crawfish and a quart of cold beer, checking your crab nets every so often, is one of life's greatest and cheapest pleasures.

On the other hand, New Orleans must be the "festival" capital of the universe. The Alligator Festival, the Jambalaya Festival, the Honduran Festival, the Shrimp Festival, the list goes on, often two or three a week to pick from.

The Jazz and Heritage Festival, two weeks long, has reached international proportions; top names in every imaginable genre: blues, jazz, gospel, cajun, zydeco, all this under tents, in the sun, cooled by March breezes and scented by the spicy aroma of boiled crawfish bubbling in cast-iron vats. Refried confusion.

The partying goes beyond the festivals. Tipitina's and other hole-in-the-wall nightclubs are scattered all over the city, with New Orleans music, dancing, listening, and lots of drinking.

New Orleans is an island, bordered by the Mississippi, Lake Pontchartrain, marshes and bayous. Fishing, canoeing, sailboat racing are year-round pursuits readily and cheaply available.

(At the New Orleans School of Cooking, at the Jackson Brewery, there's a three-hour class in authentic creole cooking, weaving Indian, French, Spanish and African styles. In a sociable atmosphere, the charge for Joe Cahn's class is listed as only $15, and that includes a full-course meal with beer as a topper.

On a visit through the narrow twisting pathways of the St. Louis Cemetery, with its eerie above-ground vaults, one can see the grave of the famous psychic, Marie Laveau.)

Positive-Expectation Gambling (2 pts)

G.M.: Generations of sophisticated, gentleman gamblers have been practicing their craft at Fair Grounds race track for over 100 years. General George Armstrong Custer owned and operated a winning stable here before shipping out and losing a decision to Sitting Bull. There are three other racetracks in the state which keep local off-track-betting parlors open on a year-round basis.

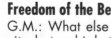

Freedom of the Bedroom (2 pts)

G.M.: What else would you expect from a tropical city but a high tolerance for sexual matters and personal preferences? You can feel the sexy, steamy atmosphere. Walk down Decauter Street on a spring night with a big hazy white moon hanging over the river. It's muggy. The air is sticky and thick. A big cockroach scampers across the sidewalk into the gutter and you suddenly look up. There she is...a beautiful woman, barefoot, with pierced earrings, a flower print dress, sitting by a fountain, fanning herself with a wide palmetto leaf. Fantasy? Maybe. Maybe not.

It was not an accident that *A Streetcar Named Desire* was written here. A high visibility and feeling for things sensual and erotic exist here. Let's put it another way—the Osmond family would not fit in to the scene.

(The New Orleans City Council passed a comprehensive measure to ban discrimination based on sexual orientation, the only deep-south city to do so.)

G.M.: Where else can you see men in a supermarket drinking a beer as they push the basket? Where else could you see two cars stopped at a traffic light and the occupants of both vehicles carrying on a conversation even as the light flashes green? These are real stories from a city that I have come to love.

TOTAL POINTS: 39

NEW PALTZ, NEW YORK

Woodstock hogs all the attention, but in its shadow, nearby New Paltz has been the site of a true ongoing regeneration of various counterculture periods of the past. The off-beat began brewing more than three decades ago on New Paltz's State University of New York campus, where the art department was planting the seeds of the college's non-conformist, rebellious character.

During those years, the "townies" and the students existed on two different channels, mingling occasionally at a pool table or bar. But gradually, small town and campus have converged into one consolidated but multifaceted contrarian experience. Part of this transformation was catalyzed when an unusually large proportion of students decided to remain in the small town after graduating.

Upended Facilities (1 of 3 pts)

An example of this merger is a local horse ranch that offers horses and teachers for one of the credit Phys-Ed courses. The old campus dining hall has been turned into a summer theater attracting residents from beyond the campus.

Other structural transmutations include the old Shell Station, which is now a fruit and vegetable market, and two indoor gyms used for rock climbing exercises.

Unconventional Regional Customs (5 of 6 pts)

Effectively, what began on the campus is now the general characteristic of the town. One need only walk down the main drag in order to see weird people hanging out. One bearded guy is dressed in an outfit composed of a collage of homemade medals. He's been standing out there for years.

On the curb steps in front of Hoffman's Delicatessen and Home Cooking sat a few punkers blending in with other people, normal in appearance, who lingered there as if the street were their living room.

One long-time New Paltz resident explained that the town is a mecca for strange people of different persuasions. No one will feel out of place. There is no one strange custom, since so many people are weird in their very own way.

At Barner Books, by the cash register, a copy of Kerouac's *On The Road* is the only conspicuous book display. I asked the manager what was selling best at his store. "The Beats," he said.

"What else?" I asked. He mulled over my question.

"The Beats. They're our best sellers."

Various local enterprises seem to be in business for social reasons as much as for profits. For example, if you deal with Manny at "Manny's" funky art supply store, prepare yourself for elaborate tales of advice and wisdom.

New Paltz's more subterranean culture has been featured in an obscure novel called *The Golden Fleece*.

Cross-Cultural (3 of 5 pts)

No region of the country is more "middle America" than upstate New York. This makes the significant presence of various cultures and lifestyles in New Paltz more striking. African Americans and other so-called minorities are a part of the fabric of the town. New Agers, gays, health-food junkies, jocks, and Christian fundamentalists all have their own haunts.

Bizarre Geography (1 of 6 pts)

While the natural geography is not as varied as the human geography, New Paltz is located on a relatively flat plain with high rocky cliffs forming a wall at the west end of the valley, making it ideal for ballooning.

Mixed-Use Zoning (2 of 3 pts)

The streets are asymmetrical, both horizontally, with diagonals and curves, and vertically, with hills. People live right within the commercial district. At the same time, commerce spreads to areas that otherwise would be strictly residential.

There has been a disturbing growth of malls and mini-malls between the town and the New York State Thruway, leaving the main entrance to New Paltz in a strip-mall-America mode.

Alternative Economy (3 points)

One resident described the economy of New Paltz as bottom-up. There was once a furniture enterprise called "Shady Deals". It may still exist, although it has no address by which to trace it. It would pop up at auctions and social events.

There is a farmers market just outside of town, and several street vendors within. More inherent to the town are hundreds of little enterprises that thrive in an alternative economy thanks to the non-mainstream lifestyles and consuming habits that provide a market.

The Wildflower restaurant, for example, a vegetarian haunt, began on a shoestring, with dishes that didn't match, and chairs of distinct shapes and forms. Locals and students work side by side in establishments such as this one.

Former radicals who would be frowned upon by the corporate economy seem to find their niche in New Paltz.

Many local enterprises sell unique, homemade items unheard of at regional malls. One-of-a-kind jewelry, for example, can be found at The Callaloo Shop, as well as hand-painted pillows and many locally exclusive items created by regional artists.

Pedestrian Friendly (4 of 5 pts)

If you live in town, you can get everywhere without a car. The town is compact. More important, with alternative commerce, strange people, mixed-use zoning and odd street configurations, the street acts as a magnet and becomes a happy extension of one's home.

Gentrification will never turn New Paltz into a Berkeley or a Princeton. While it has its share of upscale spots, it is basically a mellow little town with various Huguenot stone-facade buildings as a backdrop for colorful, but not chic, street life.

Non-Mainstream Entertainment (2 of 5 pts)

The cliffs surrounding New Paltz are filled with rock climbers. In fact, New Paltz is to rock climbing what Aspen is to skiing, with several shops that specialize in this sport.

Other local traditions include ballooning and on-campus alternative theater.

Positive-Expectation Gambling (1 of 2 pts)

A small off-track betting establishment provides horse race wagering on New York tracks. A distinct sub-culture hangs out here. While some of the original beatniks were horseplayers, the nouveau beats of New Paltz have largely ignored this small OTB, which is concealed from the main drag by an office building.

Recommended eating: the mushroom-avocado burrito at Baccus, the vegetarian dishes at the Wildflower Restaurant, and the great atmosphere at the Main Street Bistro, where you can eat to the sound of clanking plates and look down upon hardwood floors that are in dire need of sanding. If you like the combination of greasy spoon and gourmet, this is your place. The international menu even includes a medieval artichoke dish called Carcofi. And there's gourmet coffee to top off the meal.

The Main Course offers the best value in bistro cooking, while Conca d'oro is usually brimming with people, all of whom will be smelling of garlic by the time they finish their tasty Italian food.

New Paltz has more bars than churches, and the night life spills out into the streets.

TOTAL POINTS: 22

NEW YORK MILLS, MINNESOTA

New York Mills is the home of the annual Great American Think-off, this nation's only philosophy competition, as well as a thriving regional arts center, surprisingly situated in the proverbial middle of nowhere.

Non-Mainstream Recreation (3 of 5 pts)

The long, bitter winters with howling winds and cruel blizzards may be partly responsible for making this town philosophical about life. The Great American Think-off has been a competitive duel in which 728 people from 46 states face off on philosophical questions. The competition is expanding to attract national participation. When it gets down to the "Final Four," the audience is packed.

The 1994 final was based on the question: does life have meaning? Heavy stuff. If they held the competition in the middle of winter, the contestants might come up with different, more sobering answers. One of the finalists in the 1994 Think-Off was a former professional gambler; another, a Zen Buddhist monk from Coon Rapids, Iowa. The winner of the final match is decided by audience vote.

The winner, by a close margin, maintained that there is a meaning to life. The runner-up, the monk, said that life simply "is."

Awards to winners included cash and medals showing Rodin's "Thinker" seated on a tractor.

With the event blacked out from local TV, more than one-tenth of the town's inhabitants attended. Although the event was not covered by ESPN, National Public Radio did a story on it.

In the 1993 competition, the audience ended up split down the middle on the question of whether human beings are basically good or evil. The 1995 topic: Money vs. Morality. Which does society value more?

Unconventional Regional Customs (4 of 6 pts)

Mills is not a one-event town. The New York Mills Regional Cultural Center, housed in an 1885 building, hosts events in jazz, film, literature, visual arts, and poetry, with a distinct slant toward making the arts part of everyday lives of the country folk in the area. In fact, one upcoming event is a Farmer's Poetry Contest.

The Center's artists-in-residence program, a juried affair, demands that the artists descend from their ivory tower. In fact, the ivory tower around these parts is more likely to be a grain elevator. One of the 1994 artists was a painter of grain elevators, the American equivalent of the French chateaux. Another artist painted portraits of local nursing home residents. Still others brought their skills into the schools. One of the seven invited artists came all the way from France.

The town has a high per capita population of artists, but art and family farming are not seen as separate ways of life, and art itself has a progressive definition that embraces all types of creative endeavors.

Pedestrian Friendly (2 of 4 pts)

Nearer to Fargo, North Dakota than to Minneapolis, New York Mills, affectionately known as Mills, is far enough removed from the Interstate to have escaped the shopping mall phenomenon. As a result, it has a living downtown, quite appealing for pedestrians.

The small size of the town means that sooner or later, residents with wanderlust will have need for a car. However, most important commerce is within walking distance, including two food stores and a couple of hardware stores. As clothing stores move out of most small towns, one recently moved into New York Mills.

Meanwhile, the commercial setting is of older, historic buildings, with the only exceptions being the new Eagles Café and the Public Library.

Add to the equation a friendly population and you have an ideal place to handle both business and pleasure on foot. If you're thinking of moving there, it's possible to find a well-insulated three-bedroom home in the $30,000 range.

Mixed-Use Zoning (1 of 4 pts)
Should you want to live right in downtown, you may have the good fortune to find a vacant apartment above the chiropractor's office, or at least on a side street within short range of the commercial center.

Public Hangouts (1 of 5 pts)
Tiny New York Mills will never rival New Orleans or Berkeley in the realm of public hangouts, but it has its spots. Artists and other townies hang out regularly at Muggs Pub, and the bakery now has a pleasant deli section where regulars sip coffee and chat. The Blue Horizon Ballroom is open weekend nights.

Alternative Economy (1 of 3 pts)
While you won't find street vendors in February, the town has created one positive void in the economy, a climate (don't take me literally) conducive for selling one's art and handcrafted work. Along with two ongoing galleries, hundreds of artists and craftspeople sell their creations at the annual Continental Divide Music and Film Festival, on the third weekend in July at Smith Park.

And with no mall nearby, ma and pa still have a chance to make it in the business world.

Cross-Cultural (1 of 5 pts)
You can hear a Lutheran service in the Finnish language, and many homes still have authentic Finnish saunas.

New York Mills is a town with a positive and very distinct spirit. Unlike much of small town Minnesota, Mills has not needed to merge with other municipalities.

Thanks in part to the efforts of cultural center coordinator John P. Davis, philosophical New York Mills asks questions about its existence. Enough answers have emerged so that this tiny dot on the map has a bold-mark impact on the world.

TOTAL POINTS: 13

NOME, ALASKA

Any town that hosts the Bering Sea Ice Golf Classic and the Labor Day Bathtub Race must have a few weird people in it. Alaska has become "a collection point for an odd assortment of misfits, outcasts, adventurers, escapists, opportunists, wanderers, malcontents and rootless folks just plain weary of civilization's restraints and predictability," according to David Lamb.

Lamb writes that in Nome, "the entire population still turns over every nine years."

Bizarre Geography (5 of 6 pts)

You can't get to Nome by car, not even from other cities in Alaska. This city's airport offers no direct flights to New York or Washington D.C. but you can fly directly to Provideniya, Siberia, only 190 miles away. Although Privideniya is but an hour away, you'll be flying into tomorrow as you cross the international dateline.

In December, you can be a night owl for 20 hours but on June 21, you can celebrate the Midnight Sun Festival in 21½ hours of daylight.

From November to March, on clear nights, if you're willing to go out in the bitter cold, you'll be rewarded with the spectacular Aurora Borealis, known commonly as the Northern Lights.

Over 200 species of wildflowers grow on the nearby Seward Peninsula between June and August. During this period, you can expect a low of 32°F and a high of 75°F.

The ultimate geographic curiosity of the Nome region is its gold, easily found, but requiring supreme patience in panning.

Unconventional Regional Customs (4 of 6 pts)

Every summer, miners still travel to Nome to live on the beach and search for gold.

Meanwhile, some intrepid youngsters actually go swimming in the frigid Bering waters.

Native cultures in the surrounding region maintain a tradional subsistence lifestyle, based on hunting and fishing.

Outsiders settle in Nome because it is the last frontier, the ultimate hiding place or the paramount test of endurance.

Cross-Cultural (3 of 6 pts)

Eskimo customs survive to a far greater extent in Nome than they do in larger Alaska cities; native Alaskan food preparation, art and clothing are evident on a daily basis. Among the various art forms are ivory carvings from walrus tusks. The Eskimo population makes up about 54 percent of

Nome's 4,500 inhabitants. There are three distinct cultural groups of Alaska Native Eskimos in the Bering Strait Region. Eskimo delicacies such as walrus, seal and whale (muktuk) are available to the public.

Public Hangouts (2 of 5 pts)

You won't find outdoor espresso cafes, but Nome's saloon culture dates back to Gold Rush times and is still alive and jumping. Residents will often remark that Nome's eight saloons do a lot more business than her thirteen churches. The adjective most often used when referring to these hangouts is "infamous." Wyatt Earp ran the Dexter Saloon for three years but the tough winters finally softened him up and he retreated to California.

Mixed-Use Zoning (3 of 4 pts)

While most of the bars are located the waterfront area, in and around Front Street, everything else is scattered about in unplanned fashion. Numerous streets end in T-junctions, something that utilitarian urban planners frown upon. In cold climates, T-junctions minimize the wind-tunnel effect you'd get in streets that have no obstructions.

Pedestrian Friendly (1 of 4 pts)

Everything in Nome is within walking distance, and there are a few interesting old Gold Rush buildings surviving the city's fires and floods, but there are too many days when it's too darn cold to be out there for a stroll, even if you dress in layers, as is the custom in these parts.

Non-Mainstream Recreation (5 pts)

For those who can take the cold, there is a wide array of activities available, thanks to Nome's funky imagination. The Bering Sea Ice Golf Classic is played on the Sunday closest to St. Patrick's Day on a six-hole par-41 golf course. Instead of sand traps, there are bothersome chunks of ice. Imagine searching for a stray white ball on the white ice. The tournament organizers solved that problem by putting orange golf balls into play. You may use a dogsled to get from hole to hole.

There are day and overnight flights to Siberia for about $500 round trip, less expensive if by group charter. You might find a cheaper flight through Russian airlines, Aeroflot. The flight takes an hour and twenty minutes. The Siberian town Provideniya is known for its hospitality.

The Midnight Sun Festival goes on for a week, from sunup to sundown, which means for nearly 24 hours a day. The festival features the Midnight Sun Softball Tournament, Nome's raunchy version of the World Series.

Labor Day festivities include the Bathtub Race. Racing bathtubs must be full of water at the outset of the race and have at least ten gallons of water left in them by the finish line. Meanwhile, at least one member of each racing team must be in the bathtub-on-wheels during the race.

The beaches in Nome may not rival Maui's, but they offer abundant driftwood, easily used for a cooking fire or bonfire. A Nome-style picnic consists of catching your dinner in the river and cooking it on the beach.

Nome's greatest claim to fame is the Iditarod Trail Sled Dog Race, departing in Anchorage and fittingly ending in Nome. Initiated in 1925, when a dog team carried serum to treat a diptheria epidemic, this event is considered along with the Kentucky Derby and the Tour de France as one of the world's greatest races!

For spectators, the Iditarod may be the most satisfying of the three. The Derby offers about two minutes and two seconds of inspiring drama after weeks of foreplay. The Tour de France ends with 8 laps in and around the Champs Elysees. But the Iditarod's prolonged climax lasts for a period of a week and a half in the month of March, as the teams' mushers reach the finish line.

The Iditarod festivities consist of a 50-team basketball tournament, the Ice Golf Classic and numerous other events, including a chance to "meet the mushers" and congratulate them on their arrival. The festival winds down after nearly a month.

Alternative Economy (2 of 3 pts)

For tourists, gold panning is purely recreational but for some diehards, it represents an alternative livelihood. Large quantities of gold can be discovered on the beaches and in the hills and ravines; but much larger volumes of gravel must be "washed out" in order to make a living wage. It's a labor-intensive occupation.

No permit is required for panning, but the panner must take care not to encroach on land that is part of existing claims. Proper pans are available in local stores. Advice on the best panning spots is sometimes available.

If you plan to take your gold mining seriously, you might avoid the pitfalls that beset Charlie Chaplin by seeking advice from the Gold Prospectors Association of America, P.O. Box 891509, Temecula, CA 92589 (phone 909/699-4749).

Alaska is an expensive region but Nome has some reasonably priced places to bed down. Betty's Igloo is a Bed & Breakfast with a $55 rate for singles and $70 for two, including breakfast (907/443-2419). Weeks Apartments, offers daily, weekly and monthly rates. One bedroom for a month runs $35 a day (P.O. Box 421, Nome, AK 99762). Representative food prices are: chicken, $1.79 lb.; potatoes, $5.69 per 10-lb. bag; eggs, $1.89 dozen; bananas, $.99 lb.

Many Alaskans visit Hawaii in the winter. I wonder why? Those who are obligated to stay not only face the bitter cold but must contend with SAD, seasonal affective disorder. These mid-winter blues are a depression-like condition brought on by the lack of light. I asked Cynthia, a native of Nome, how she contended with the prolonged darkness.

"For those of us who were raised here," she said, "it doesn't have that great an effect."

From March to August, at least, there's no place like Nome.

TOTAL POINTS: 25

NOTSOSOHO, NEW YORK

Soho stands for "South of Houston" Street. It is an extension of Manhattan's Greenwich Village. Its old factories and warehouses have been refurbished by affluent artists. By our guidelines, Soho is probably too chic to be rated here, but just to its north (NOT) and its south (SO), the chic affluence is dispersed into communities of broader economic and social dimensions. Hence, we have Notsosoho.

As historic buildings continue their facelifts and galleries and restaurants add more nuances of elegance, Soho is becoming an art ghetto. Even outdoor produce stands must arrange their fruit in the dazzling layout of a brilliant collage. It would be a crime to bite into the sculpted bread sold at the Vesuvius Bakery. (On seeing the display window, I first thought I was looking into another art gallery.)

I had been yearning for a cup of espresso. I came across an outdoor café with a free table; but as I observed the hip people dressed in black at the other tables, there flashed an invisible sign: reserved for artist. Even in the comparable Marais district of Paris, one can find café-bars with a more varied clientele, Côtes du Rhone proletarians among them.

Soho has all the ingredients of a dynamic community, **public hangouts** galore (5 pts), a totally **pedestrian friendly** ambience with historic buildings looking down on cobblestone streets (4 pts), **mixed-use zoning** (4 pts) with commerce and residence (quite expensive, of course) on the same blocks and in the same buildings, and **upended facilities** (3 pts) with its famous conversions of warehouses into artists' lofts.

But the monolithic class structure seems to create an invisible imperviousness, not only for non-artists but perhaps for starving artists, as well. In one gallery, a sign: "Money Creates Taste," while a block north of Canal Street, on Wooster, a crude hand poster featuring a gun with the words, "Kill All Artists."

Just north of Soho, and just to the south as well, the neighborhoods display positive features similar to Soho, while retaining a more varied cultural and economic base. Lining the north border between Soho and Greenwich Village, along Houston, is an array of street vendors, with the Ecuadorians who sell sheep wool sweaters looking no different than the folks I had once seen at the outdoor market in Otavalo, Ecuador.

The ribbon that separates the south end of Soho from Tribeca is lined with flea market enterprises along Canal Street. All that is cheap and not artistic is for sale; the scene is fitting of an offbeat, three-dimensional mural.

The **alternative economy** is alive and well both north and south of Soho (3 pts). If they're not hawking something, then they're doing other outdoor acts, mainly in Washington Square, which still retains its anarchist spirit. Within the myriad of clubs, there are still a few where up-and-coming artists can break in. The Nuyorican Poets Cafe's multicultural offerings include "poetry slams" where the best poet always loses, one-act plays such as "Men Don't Cry," and many more surprises. Café Sin-é (Gaelic for "That's It") holds spontaneous, unorganized jam sessions, including singer-songwriter material.

The cultural variety of entertainment, food and local commerce in these neighborhoods is staggering (**cross-cultural** 3 of 5 pts).

The Village I used to enjoy continues to evolve, as I witnessed with sadness when I passed the boarded-up Village Gate. Also gone is the Five Spot, where I regularly heard Thelonius Monk. But other jazz clubs I remember from the time I was growing up are still there, including the venerable Village Vanguard.

After having zigzagged through Soho, still yearning for my espresso, I was distracted by a nostalgic scene from my youth. Just outside Soho, a few yards from Canal Street, there was a pick-up basketball game in a typical cement park cramped into a tiny triangle of real estate. I remembered that the street life in New York is as varied and textured as anywhere in the USA.

Forget the espresso, I thought. I went into a honky tonk luncheonette and asked for a coffee. It was a test. It used to be they would automaticly serve coffee with cream unless you specified otherwise. Sure enough, the coffee came over the counter with cream, and for once, it tasted better than the café latté I could have had a few blocks north.

Unconventional Regional Customs (4 of 6 pts)

Non-conformists have historically gravitated to Greenwich Village. In an area where the arts are mainstream, creativity spills over into other fields. New York's new system of alternative schools may represent the best answer yet to the notorious problems of contemporary public eduction. While not all is rosy with the experiment, the initial progress reports are quite positive. In particular, right here in Tribeca (south of Soho) is the Wildcat Academy (sounds like a better name than Jefferson High). Most of the 120 students in the school were truants elsewhere, and a fourth of them are on probation or parole.

The school is on the sixth floor of a former paper warehouse on Hudson Street. With its rigidly structured, but at the same time nurturing atmosphere, the Wildcat Academy is enabling students who would not have made it elsewhere to find an avenue to success.

Both north and south of Soho (Notsosoho), the street life is spirited and the neighborhoods offer a great deal more than animated yuppie entertainment scenes. With OTBs and race tracks not far away (2 pts) and a comprehensive set of laws banning discrimination based on sexual preference (2 pts), this area in the heart of New York continues to cultivate free spirits.

TOTAL POINTS: 30

COKE, NORTH CAROLINA

Ocracoke Island has been migrating toward the mainland of North Carolina and within the next eon might reach the coast. In the meantime, in spite of an influx of tourists, it remains out of the mainstream of life in the USA.

Bizarre Geography (3 of 6 pts)

With no highway to Ocracoke Village, the ferry is the best way to reach the island. Thanks to isolation, the locals' dialect maintains traces of the Elizabethan English of its early settlers, the most infamous of whom was Edward Teach, better known as Blackbeard.

This sea-level village has often been in the direct path of thrashing hurricanes, but somehow the community has held firm. The history of Ocracoke might be written from the point of view of numerous shipwrecks, which left all kinds of salvage material. In fact, the wooden cross at the Methodist Church was carved from a piece of sunken freighter.

Unconventional Regional Customs (3 of 6 pts)

The island's isolation has contributed to its fierce community spirit and make-do ingenuity. For example, until recently, there was no doctor in town. That meant that Ocracokers delivered each other's babies and attended to their own illnesses with various home remedies, some of which remain in use today. Some folks still make and use blueberry wine, for example, to treat diarrhea and upset stomach.

It's not as if the residents of this fishing-village-turned-tourist-retreat were self-consciously trying to be different. The mainstream simply never flowed close enough to have a great impact. As a result, most of what we know of the shopping mall, fast food culture has made no inroads on the island. Needless to say, there are no water slides on the beach.

Even excesses of the modern funeral industry have made little impact on the island, thanks to the Ocracoke Burial Association; when someone dies, each member contributes thirty cents to help the family with funeral expenses. There are fifteen small cemeteries along the funky East Howard Street.

Pedestrian Friendly (4 pts)

East Howard Street is one of the main roads to the beach, yet it remains unpaved. Alton Ballance's fine book, *Ocracokers*, gives us an image of this street: "Steady traffic has pressed the sand and dust hard, forming two ruts that wind past old houses, tiny graveyards, ancient live oaks...fences are so close to the sandy lane that you can reach out and touch some of them as you drive through."

Everyone we spoke to agreed that it is easier and more interesting to get around Ocracoke Village on foot or on a bicycle. You would then have a better view of those old houses along East Howard Street, including the ones that still have detached kitchens.

Mixed-Use Zoning (4 pts)

While East Howard Street is one of the few places that retain the look of Ocracoke the way it used to be, the town's opposition to modern zoning laws has left it entirely mixed use. That means more sensorial pleasure for the pedestrian.

In April of 1986, faced with an influx of home buyers, some of them speculators, and with resulting higher taxes threatening the quality of life of long-time residents, the town passed a controlled growth ordinance.

"Unlike many zoning ordinances," writes Ballance, who was County Commissioner at the time, "the Ocracoke ordinance is intended to allow all uses, both commercial and residential, anywhere within the village."

Alternative Economy (1 of 3 pts)

As tourism replaces fishing as the dominant economy, Ocracoke remains a fishing village. Mullet fishing in shallow waters from skiffs sounds like an honest profession, or at least a great way to spend the day.

Meanwhile, tourism brings local craftspeople a market for their goods, adding a vital dimension to the island's economy.

While residents may complain of changing times, many stores still maintain the old customs. The Community Store, for example, sells everything "from screwdrivers to sherbet," and has a community bulletin board outside.

The micro-business world of Ocracoke remains unchained to the mainland.

Public Hangouts (1 of 5 pts)

Outside the Community Store are benches for sitting and chatting. Various local restaurants, none of them chains, offer good food at moderate prices with a homespun atmosphere conducive to sticking around.

Non-Mainstream Recreation (2 of 5 pts)

Blackbeard's hidden treasure has never been found. Statistically there is a better probability of finding the Blackbeard cache than of hitting a state lottery.

Pony pens just outside the town are the home for some two dozen wild ponies. Should you take your kids to watch them, keep them at a safe distance on the lookout deck. These are not domesticated animals.

Ballance's oral history of Ocracoke was written out of fear that a way of life may soon be lost, but he also implied that outsiders are not in control of the future. "I think you have to spend a year at Ocracoke just listening," says one resident, "before you start inflicting."

Ocracoke's distinctive traits make it a great deal more engaging than a village of its size should be. It did not have any kind of communication with the outside world until World War II, when it housed a navy base. Yet, it was closer to that decisive period in history than any large city on the continent; residents actually watched as German submarines sank merchant ships and tankers off the coast. No wonder the town acquired the nickname Torpedo Junction.

Traditionally, it has maintained a type of libertarian welfare system. "We have a structure here," said one resident, "of taking care of people without the need of a lot of agencies...almost everybody has someone that takes care of them."

The ferry from Hatteras to Ocracoke is free. There are also toll ferries from the mainland. There are no bridges projected in the near future and that bodes well for Ocracoke retaining a good deal of its local flavor.

TOTAL POINTS: 18

PARK CITY, UTAH

Yes, Park City is a four-season resort, noted most for its skiing and natural beauty. However, it is also a town of many other dimensions, some of them quite unique. In particular, it is the site, for ten days every January, of the Sundance Film Festival, a most noted forum for independent film makers, initiated by Robert Redford in 1981.

"The people participating in the festival are not your typical visitors," said one resident. "We call them 'The people wearing black,' and we try to wear black those days ourselves."

Park City's history is unlike that of any other Utah town. From mining town with 27 saloons and a wild red-light district, to ghost town, to recreation center, Park City is one of the few places in Utah with non-sectarian roots.

Recent reports tell of an influx of wealthy home buyers that has driven up the value of real estate and threatens to price out the lower economic echelons of the city. But Park City has come up with some proactive measures. An "affordable housing task force" and the introduction of 94 low income units for purchase or as rentals proves that the town is anxious to hold on to its character.

Unlike parallel resort towns, Park City strives to be a place to live, not just to visit. Fifty-six percent of its service employees are still able to live in the city itself rather than commuting from cheaper areas. This is a high percentage when compared to other resorts.

Mixed-Use Zoning (4 pts)

There are 84 buildings in town listed on the national register of historic places. A number of these structures house retail shops at street level and rental housing on the second and third floors. Beyond the Main Street core is what they call a transitional zone, which is struggling to come up with the proper mix of residential and commercial property, but meanwhile remains a spirited place to take a walk.

The city's visionary planning director is referred to as "the city shrink." He is against converting the Main Street core into a pedestrian mall. Streets without vehicles lose a vital dimension. So long as storefronts reach the street and there are no mini-mall parking lots, street parking in front of stores adds texture to the atmosphere of a downtown.

Upended Facilities (3 pts)

The vintage Miners Hospital was restored more than a decade ago and converted to a public library. "More than 700 Parkites formed a human book brigade and transferred hundreds of volumes from the old facility to the new."

But then, the library outgrew its facility and was moved to a converted school. Meanwhile the Miners Hospital is now called "the community living room," where people show up to read magazines and where community events are held.

Other conversions: an old limestone school house into an inn (a half block from Main Street), another old school house into City Hall, and original miners' shacks to residences and summer retail sites, thanks to a matching grant program.

Public Hangouts (2 of 4 pts)

Any town that can create a community living room must have an inherent affinity for hangouts, and most coffee shops and restaurants in town do not have a modern, in-and-out philosophy.

Pedestrian Friendly (2 of 4 pts)

Out west, with the immense distances, one is obligated to own and use a car. Nevertheless, the main street charm of Park City makes it a pleasing place to walk. There is a plan "afoot" outlining master trails for joggers, pedestrians and bicyclists, which makes sense, since fitness is a cultural priority in Park City.

Cross-Cultural (1 of 5 pts)

Everyone knows that Utah is a predominantly white, English speaking state. But Park City's history was one of ethnic diversity, and in spite of the fact that it is 95 percent white, it just elected the first black city council member in the whole state of Utah.

"We may not be diverse," said one resident, "but we're not a closed community."

Unconventional Regional Customs (1 of 6 pts)

One would not expect the arts to be so pervasive in a mountain ski town; yet, there are 14 galleries for only 6,000 permanent residents. With schools of a more traditional three-Rs bent, the Park City Arts Council does much to bring the arts to children, through puppeteers, childrens' theater, story tellers, and dancers, with functions held in school auditoriums.

Meanwhile, a "Music-in-the-Mountains" program attempts to

schedule a different outdoor concert every day during the summer.

Bizarre Geography (1 of 6 pts)
Park City's Uinta Mountains are the only mountain range in North America that goes east-west, as opposed to north-south.

Thanks to the art galleries, and other destination-retail operations, commerce in the city proper has felt a minimum impact from a regional mall six miles away. A seductive array of restaurants has also helped keep people in town.

Claimjumper (Steak and Potatoes), Adolph's (European), Cicero's (Italian) and Baja Cantina(Mexican) are recommended by locals for good eats.

TOTAL POINTS: 14

PORTLAND, OREGON

P ortland, Oregon is one of those few urban centers that has worked hard at nurturing a city-wide sense of place. At a time, about three decades ago, when many major U.S. cities were being defaced by urban renewal and deflated by flight to the suburbs, Portland's eccentric city planning in retrospect seems so sensible.

Unconventional Regional Customs (5 of 6 pts)
In the early 1970s, a study called for 10,000 more downtown parking spaces in order to support the expanding economy. Most other U.S. cities had similar studies and followed through on them. Portland went the other way, opting in favor of more efficient mass transit.

At that time, it was downright countercultural to forge a public policy that went against automobile and oil-company interests. "If any place has a chance to do things differently and get it right," writes Phillip Langdon in the *The New Yorker*, "Portland is it."

Actually, a whole collage of contrarian public-policy moves led to the composite picture of Portland today. While other cities were putting in freeways, Portland removed its riverfront expressway and replaced it with a park. Denouncing "coastal condomania," Tom McCall helped get the state to begin requiring urban areas to establish "growth boundaries," similar to what was done in Burlington, Vermont, in order to ward off the "ravenous rampage of suburbia."

As we shall see, these public policies have engendered a number of spicy idiosyncrasies in Portland. But before we get to these, here are a few more weird customs. The Portland area has two parks with nudist sectors: Rooster Rock, 20 miles east on I-84 and Sauvie Island, one of the largest river islands in the States, only 15 minutes from downtown Portland. (Unspoiled Sauvie Island also features U-Pick Fruit operations.)

Symbolic support of nudism is the bronze, nude statue commemorating Bud Clark's pose as a flasher in the "Expose Yourself to Art" poster. The poster came out some time before the ex-tavern owner was elected Mayor in 1985 in what was to become a two-term stay in office. Bearded Clark would ride to work on a bike, more symbolism that the automobile is no icon in Portland.

The statue is found at the attractive, brick-street Transit Mall. A 300-block area of downtown Portland is known as Fareless Square because you can ride a Tri-Met bus or MAX light rail car for free.

Downtown fishing is proof that Portland can keep the small town in the big city. America's largest forested municipal park, modestly named Forest Park, is more evidence that Portland has also been able to keep the country in the city. Visitors must share the park with elk and their ilk.

Finally, Portland's famous Rose Festival (June) was countered with an anti-Rose Queen protest. But in 1994, the Rose Festival responded with its own feminist medicine. The new queen did not fit the stereotype of the sculpted supermodel. She was chosen in part for a different reason. She was the place kicker for the Lincoln High boy's football team, the first football player ever named queen of a beauty pageant!

Pedestrian Friendly (4 pts)

Visionary public policy has made Portland one of the few pedestrian friendly cities in the USA. A good portion of downtown is paved or sidewalked in various brick hues from orange to maroon. The rough feeling of brick under auto wheels is an admonishment to drivers that the city cares for pedestrians.

To combat typical sensory deprivation that plagues downtowns, Portland insisted that new buildings, including parking garages, have stores or other pedestrian-attracting uses at street level.

Thanks to the park replacing the freeway, the downtown was reunited with its riverfront. Meanwhile, the state and city have both passed laws to ensure public art displays, with 1.33 percent of construction costs going to art. The result is a continuing feast for the eyes.

Pedestrian-friendliness requires support from public transportation. Besides the free-fare zone, fares to other neighborhoods are quite reasonable, a great incentive to leave the car home.

One characteristic of many downtowns that discourages people from walking around is the presence of aggressive panhandlers and the disheartening imagery of the homeless. Portland is not without this problem but deals with it in a humane way. Formerly homeless people now belong to a cleaning crew that erases patches of graffiti.

Green-jacketed Portland Guides are on the watch for street disorder. With more mellow tactics than police, these trained conflict-resolution employees try to help mentally-ill street people and panhandlers with "can we get you some food?" When things get hairy, "a persistent panhandler may be discouraged by guides who stand on both sides of him or her, doing paperwork."

There is also a small corps of armed patrol officers who do not make arrests but who can be at the scene "in an average of three minutes."

Public Hangouts (5 pts)

Lively hangouts are inherent to Portland's cityscape. Most celebrated is Pioneer Courthouse Square, an open-air living room. Paved with red bricks, its center is a sculpted amphitheatre, ideal for music, political rallies and other outdoor events.

Tom McCall Park is another outdoor hangout, especially during the warmer months of ongoing festivals, for example, the Oregon Brewers' Festival.

Portland also has various neighborhoods beyond downtown with funky places to sit back and people watch. Nob Hill is Portland's Greenwich Village but the raunchier Hawthorne District probably fits best from our perspective, with "neighborhood dives, ratty cafés, and second hand book and record stores" that add balance to the more yuppified establishments.

Bagdad Theatre and Pub sells pizza and microbeer and lets you "take the grub into the show." In the Northwest area, the Mission Theatre and Brew Pub has a similar arrangement.

Mixed-Use Zoning (4 pts)

Portland has a defined strategy for increasing the number of downtown residents and many of its neighborhoods are distinguished by the vitality typical of interaction between commerce and residence.

Upended Facilities (3 pts)

In order to achieve this goal of increasing the downtown population, the North Park blocks have been refurbished to encourage the conversion of nearby old warehouses into loft apartments. Meanwhile, in Nob Hill, especially on Northwest 23rd Avenue, shops and restaurants are housed in former victorian homes.

Most cities have a warehouse section where produce has been trucked in to be picked up by retailers. One can live in a city for years and never visit this type of district. Portland's Produce Row, on the other side of the Willamette River from downtown, has the Produce Row Café, with the city's largest selection of microbrewery beers on tap.

Alternative Economy (2 of 3 pts)

The only bad thing about Portland's alternate economy is that it is in danger of being absorbed into the mainstream. Portland's microbreweries, for example, have become a tourist attraction. Rivaling Belgium and Munich, local brew masters experiment extensively with fresh Northwest ingredients, including fruits. You can find raspberry ale, wheat beer and other exotic hand-crafted beverages. When you find a bar where the ale is produced on premises, you know it won't be of the corporate variety.

Meanwhile, Portland's Saturday Market, an open-air bazaar in the Skidmore Historic District, offers 250 open-air booths of ethnic food and obscure crafts, with street entertainers around Skidmore Fountain.

Positive-Expectation Gambling (1 pt of 2)

At Portland Meadows Race Track, bottom-of-the-barrel thoroughbreds compete to see which is big fish in the small pond of racing. Watch the toteboard. Insider action is important here.

Non-Mainstream Entertainment (2 of 5 pts)

Most larger cities have a wide array of fine entertainment and Portland is no exception. Compared with festivals from other cities, Portland's are neither more nor less unusual. The difference is that Portland provides the congenial setting and the mild climate to make you want to go.

Among the ones that seem the most outlandish are Artquake (September at Pioneer Square), Nehalem Duck Days (Winter, featuring games and crafts related to ducks), Oregon Brewers Festival (July, with 46 independent brewers at the McCall Waterfront Park), Native American Pow Wow (June, Delta Park), and jazz and blues festivals in various settings, including waterfront, zoo, parks and under the St. Johns Bridge.

One of the funkier places to visit is the Church of Elvis, a small shop open 24 hours. Its operator, Stephanie Pierce, has performed marriage ceremonies for weird couples. She was kicked out of the annual Rose Festival for exhibiting a photograph of a penis, with the caption, "Sexism Rears Its Ugly Head."

Then there's Darcelle XV, an "entertaining" showcase of glamorous female impersonators, featuring the host and local celebrity Darcelle her/himself.

Bizarre Geography (2 of 6 pts)

At any moment, Portland could erupt. Spectacular Mount Hood, strikingly visible from downtown Portland, is not an extinct volcano, only dormant. If Mount St. Helens could do it, why not Mount Hood? The "Hood to Coast Relay," (August), sounds like our kind of race since it's mostly downhill, beginning at the top of Mount Hood. Imagine how fast the race would be run if the participants suddenly realized the volcano was beginning to erupt!

Portland is less than 80 miles from the rugged Pacific Coast. North Coast Astoria was the first American settlement west of the Rockies. Rising above victorian-era homes and an active port, the Astor Column offers unparalleled views of the six-mile wide mouth of the Columbia River, the bay and the coastal range.

Back near Portland, at the confluence of Columbia and Willamette Rivers, there's superb trout and salmon fishing off the Ross Island Bridge.

In order to protect and nurture its remarkable setting, Portland had to make certain economic sacrifices. It now seems that the loss of quick returns is going to create a scenario for long term gains.

TOTAL POINTS: 28

ROGERS PARK, CHICAGO, ILLINOIS

Chicago is still largely a city of neighborhoods. Railroad tracks and freeways take on the function of medieval ramparts in defining and confining sectors of the city. Neighborhoods acquire their own unique, often intimate character. Most of the time, ethnicity is a prevailing factor in this definition. Other times, industrial or academic institutions make social class the prevailing determinant.

When in Chicago, I divided my living time between Hyde Park, where the powerful presence of the University of Chicago assures an integrated neighborhood within a larger South Side that is primarily African American, and the Pilsen neighborhood around 18th Street, mostly Mexican.

I got to know and love both of these haunts and tried my utmost to have them qualify for this book. But in the last two years of my Chicago period, I found myself gravitating to a neighborhood on the far North Side called Rogers Park.

Cross-Cultural (6 pts)

While the integration of Hyde Park was limited by its middle class character, Rogers Park's multiethnic, multiracial tenor crosses class lines, making for a more eclectic mix. Like Hyde Park, Rogers Park is bustling with students (from the merged Loyola and Mundelein universities, and nearby Northwestern, just across the city line in Evanston). Then there are Indians and Pakistanis, Jamaicans and African Americans, Poles and Russians, just a few of the peoples represented in what writer Tem Horwitz calls "a crazy quilt of cultures."

Race, ethnicity and class are not the only barriers bridged in Rogers Park. According to a 1994 article in *Chicago Magazine*, "the nation's first intergenerational community house for independent and assisted-living elderly" is opening in Rogers Park. Younger people, some of whom receive free room and board, will share the residence with seniors, assisting the elders but gaining insights from their wisdom, too.

Independent Politics (2 of 3 pts)

Adjoining the Heartland Café (7000 Glenwood) is a shop offering independent political journals, natural products, T-shirts and odd mementos. It is there that Michael James and Kathleen Hogan publish the alternative tabloid, *Heartland: A Free American Journal.* While some have given the various Heartland entrerprises (publication, shop, café) a 60's label, my reading is one of a renaissance alternative spirit that defies all stereotypes.

Referring to tenant advocacy groups that take on sundry grass roots issues and a significant contingent of old radicals who were never yuppified, I asked Michael James if the neighborhood was as independent politically as it seemed.

He corroborated my observation, adding that there are various religious organizations involved in independent community action, including the United Church of Rogers Park, the Good News Church (United Church of Christ) and a progressive Catholic girls school with its St. Scholastic Center.

Furthermore, even the Democrats who have held office are independent of the Mayor Daley machine, including County Clerk David Orr, and Alderman Joe Moore.

Public Hangouts (5 pts)

"The neighborhood," writes Horwitz, "abounds with coffee shops," many with their devoted followings. One example is the No Exit Café and Gallery, "an authentic sixties coffeehouse with folk music, jazz and great desserts." No Exit sponsors "In One Ear," an open-mike poetry series on Mondays in a homespun atmosphere of wooden tables.

Michael James' Heartland Café could be a health food restaurant, a general store and the type of raunchy, ramshackle nightclub I remember from my old neighborhood in Paris, with its unpredictable schedule of music, poetry readings and community benefits. The food defies convenient labels. Although it's often vegetarian, there's red meat, limited to farm-raised buffalos, as well as fish and poultry. Kinky sandwiches include Grilled Almond Butter-Banana and Raisin on Whole Wheat. If you like pizza but hate cholesterol, you can ask for soy based cheese on your pizza.

The flavor of the Mexican style chicken and rice, said one gourmet, seemed more Chinese than Mexican. At Heartland Café, the food is a metaphor for the neighborhood.

James has more recently opened Heartland on the Lake, what he calls "a glorified concession stand that offers healthy food."

 ## Non-Mainstream Recreation (2 of 5 pts)

While Hyde Park has The Point, a lively gathering place that juts right out onto Lake Michigan, Rogers Park has the longest stretch of beach in the city.

Urban fishing, Chicago style: in Rogers Park, use the Pratt Street Pier. The specialty is smelt. Lake Michigan smelt are seduced by the warming waters of early spring. They glide from their deeper refuge in profuse schools toward the shore to spawn.

The season lasts for approximately 30 days. The smelt hunt is a social affair and a Rite of Spring. According to writer Kevin Horan, "fishing at the lakefront, where the piers and seawalls typically rest on tall wooden pilings, is like fishing off the edge of a swimming pool. Your net is attached to a pole on the pier through a system of two lines and a pulley."

You don't catch one fish or two. You might catch fifty or a hundred. Call it unfair competition. And defying its unfortunate name, "the smell of a freshly sliced smelt is not unlike that of a cucumber." For one month in Chicago, the aroma of spring becomes intoxicated with the sweet smell of pan-frying smelt along the lake.

Back on shore there is what might be the most offbeat sports club in the country, the Heartland Athletic Club. As with the other Heartland enterprises, the unpredictable Michael James and Kathleen Hogan are co-directors.

Consider the club's four annual 5K runs.

"Running had a different vibe," says James, "before it became so commercialized and that's what we like about these races."

One of the races, purposely scheduled in February, was run in the snow. The loose footing simply added to the informal atmosphere of the race. Race officials began by playing a few bars of the Olympics theme song on kazoos.

Mixed-Use Zoning (4 pts)

Most Chicago neighborhoods are mixed-use, street-front places. You can send your kids downstairs to the neighborhood store without forcing them to walk a mile and then dodge parking lot traffic. Rogers Park is no exception.

Pedestrian Friendly (4 pts)

The streets can be both rough and charming, with older apartment buildings of character and lots of quirky storefronts. A modicum of gentrification has a stabilizing effect without the excesses that lead to the driving out of lower economic sectors of the population.

From a more bottom-up perspective, community events leave a lasting visual feast on the landscape. For example, the first annual "Artists of the Wall" competition involved more than 75 participants, from toddlers to professional artists in creating a magnificent mural on a concrete bench along the lakefront.

One can reside in Rogers Park or visit from another part of the city without being obligated to own an automobile. Public transportation is one of Chicago's greatest assets. The buses can be pretty slow, but the el and subway system rivals the efficiency of its Paris counterpart.

Positive-Expectation Gambling (2 of 2 pts)

It is somewhat of a long haul by subway and bus to Sportsmans Park or Hawthorne race tracks in Cicero to the southwest, or by train to Arlington in the Northwest suburbs, but horse race action is always available; the player can handicap the races on the bus, so the time is well spent.

Bizarre Geography (1 of 6 pts)

Chicago is one of the few cities that has a north, south and west side without an east. East is Lake Michigan. Otherwise, its gridlike regularity may be a bit too flat and symmetrical for those of us who prefer things dissonant and erratic.

That Rogers Park can maintain its non-conformity within such a tailored geography is a tribute to its citizenry.

TOTAL POINTS: 26

ROYAL OAK, MICHIGAN

D r. Jack Kevorkian may have put this home town of his on the national map but a little store on Main Street has changed the place from within. The initial impulse that sent me to Royal Oak, scene of a 1991 post office massacre, was my fascination with Doctor Death. Was there something in the ambience of this town that might have played a role in catalyzing Kevorkian's contrarian crusade?

I got there on a mellow Sunday morning, parked the car, and began to walk the town's two main streets, Main and Washington. In front of a store called Noir Leather, which had not yet opened, I encountered a young man and woman, both dressed in black. The buzzed gaze in their eyes suggested they were not your examples of normal citizens.

"Hey," I said. "I'm writing a book on unconventional places. You think this town might qualify?"

"You're in the right place," the man said, his jet black hair outshining his tight leather outfit. The woman nodded in agreement.

"I've been all over this state," he continued, "and this is THE alternative town in Michigan."

Unconventional Regional Customs (6 pts)

A café called Brazil seemed as good a place as any to hunt down a source of information. There was a tropical mural along one wall. Jutting out from the wall were deep couches with lamps and coffee tables. On the other side was a long, semi-oval bar.

I took a seat close to the street window, next to the table of a clean-cut, middle-aged man. A pony tail and a grizzly look in his eyes suggested he was a veteran of the counter culture. He was sipping coffee and reading a book. I interrupted his tranquility, asking him for some information on Royal Oak.

Bill was 52, a single parent, born originally in Royal Oak. He had left the town for San Francisco in the late sixties, and then migrated to the Pacific Northwest. He had returned to Royal Oak, liked what he saw, and set up a halfway house for recovering addicts.

"In the 50's, Royal Oak was hit hard by the malls," he began. "The downtown literally died. When I came back, I found a little coffee house on Washington and I've been sitting around watching the place change.

"A couple of bizarre, alternative shops came to town. Punk kids with mohawks began to gather around Noir Leather.

"Then there were yuppies who came into town to look at the punks, and as a result, a few places opened up to cater to the yuppies. At that time, Birmingham got too arrogant, too plastic, too

rich. People got out of there. For example, little art dealers. They came here."

What about Kevorkian? I asked. Did he have something to do with the changes?

"Kevorkian was just a part of the craziness going on. On 4th Street, a gay book shop opened up. It took a lot of persecution. Rocks in the windows, and such. They sort of dug in, created a beachhead. Now, lots of merchants here are gay."

What about the original town people? How did they react?

Public Hangouts (5 pts)

"They'd already lost their town, first to the malls, now to the shops and cafés. Hanging out with my coffee is what I like. There's no better place to do it than right here. We're on Main Street, but you'll also see lots of unusual cafés and restaurants on Washington, most of them with tables on the sidewalk."

Pedestrian Friendly (4 pts)

I had already been to Washington Street. In fact, one can easily cover the downtown and surrounding residential streets without getting in and out of a car. But there seemed to be some other missing ingredient that was preventing the downtown from becoming malled, I suggested.

"You know that Royal Oak is the only place around here with no vagrancy laws. So we have our street people. And they're pretty well assimilated. They have free showers at the YMCA and the South Oakland Shelter acts as a clearing house for 52 churches that each house the street people for one week of the year. They also hang out at the library. They're not a picturesque bunch of people, except maybe the guy who plays the sax in front of Baskin-Robbins."

Actually, that establishment and a Wendy's on the outer edge are the only parking-lot chains within downtown, so you have the store and restaurant fronts coming right up to the sidewalk; ugly parking structures and lots are largely hidden from view.

Parking is a big problem on Friday and Saturday nights but by the time this book goes to press, the town should have a shuttle trolley to bring people in from outside the town. (Adams-Morgan, in D.C., another of our funky places, is seeking a parallel solution for its parking mess.)

While we were talking, a man shuffled in, asked permission at the bar, sat down at the piano, and played some mellow jazz. Brazil becomes a jazz club on Sunday nights while Tuesday nights are reserved for psychic readings.

Following my conversation with Bill, at a different café an attractive orange-haired woman with thick strokes of dark eyeliner would corroborate Bill's analysis.

I then returned to Noir Leather to observe the kinky action. On an outside window was a poster of a near naked woman mounting a bridled man as if he were a horse, whipping him with a black glove. Soft S&M. Inside another window was a clock that didn't work and an upside-down American flag.

Non-Mainstream Entertainment (2 of 6 pts)

In a window display was a TV monitor showing a video of the store's 1992 Fetish Fashion Show, an erotic enactment with two scantily clad women (in black, of course) and a man in black underwear and chains, going through some slow-motion choreography of erotic nuances of sex and violence. It was all suggestive. The pain is greater in a Road Runner children's cartoon.

The video drew a crowd outside the window, looking in at the entertainment. (On weekend nights, there's a $1 gawking charge.)

Also taped on the window was an enlarged copy of an angry letter protesting the lewd window displays, ending with: "I will expect to see a more acceptable display by 7 April 94. If I do not, I shall pursue other avenues to accomplish this end." Six months after the letter, nothing had changed in the storefront of Noir Leather.

Two books were also displayed, one a Dr. Seuss and the other called *The House of Pain: The Strange World of Monique Von Clef, the Queen of Humiliation*.

Inside, I mingled with the black-clad, silver-chained customers. For sale were handcuffs, from $12.99 to $34.99, black lace panties and negligee, leather pants and jackets and various novelties, including bumper stickers with messages such as "Have a Hot Lunch, Eat My Shit," and "Same Shit, Different Day."

I bought a few, finally deciding against the one that said "Fuck Authority," which might go well on Dr. Kevorkian's van.

"Lost your courage, huh?" the bechained sales kid asked.

The town includes places such as an old-fashioned main-street movie house, numerous clubs such as Metropolitan Musicafé (also with black-on-black decor), an alternative record store, an Arabic grocery, a health food market, a comedy club, various odd restaurants, whimsical cafés, art galleries and antique stores, red brick mosaics implanted in sidewalks and railroad tracks that cut across the town diagonally with frequent long freights rumbling through at street level.

Cross-Cultural (1 of 5 pts)

Royal Oak's tenor has spilled over into adjoining Ferndale, just to the south. Although Royal Oak is mainly white, Ferndale is multicultural, multiracial and multi-everything else.

Positive-Expectation Gambling (2 pts)

Within fifteen minutes are two race tracks, thoroughbreds at one, harness at the other. Royal Oak is north of Detroit. A drive straight south through Detroit and over the bridge into Windsor, Ontario, will take you to a harness track offering simulcasts of thoroughbred races in various parts of the U.S. and Canada.

Freedom in the Bedroom (2 pts)

Although I failed to find a city ordinance prohibiting discrimination based on sexual orientation, the town evidently tolerates the kinky sex imagery of Noir Leather, so it would be hard to imagine any crackdowns against milder styles of sex.

Clearly, Royal Oak is a fitting context for the rebelliousness of Dr. Kevorkian.

TOTAL POINTS: 22

SANDY HOOK, NEW JERSEY

When my wife and I lived in a town just north of Barcelona, she was almost the only woman on the beach who wore a top.

There were topless grandmothers, even topless teen-age girls under the same umbrellas; fathers didn't seem to care.

"I feel like an eccentric here," my wife said.

In the States, it's no secret that our cultural attitude toward dress and undress is reserved. So visitors to Sandy Hook are usually surprised when they come across the sign: ATTENTION. BEYOND THIS POINT YOU MAY ENCOUNTER NUDE SUNBATHERS.

Unconventional Regional Customs (4 of 6 pts)

While nudist haunts are not strange to the United States, most often, they are located in remote, hard-to-find areas where "textiles," as those of us who wear clothing are called, get the feeling the place is off limits. Typically, the instructions for how to get to a nudist hangout read: "At the last source of supplies, follow turnoff east 3 or 4 miles to a fork. Turn right on the road to Payson. About 6 or 7 miles down this road is a dirt turnoff to Childs. Turn right (it is Fossil Creek Road) and follow about 17 miles to a fork and turn right, another 5 miles. This road dead-ends before Childs. Take gravel road left to Verde River. Hike one-mile-plus upstream, crossing river to old bathhouse."

No wonder there's not much interaction between nudists and textiles.

But Gunnison Beach at Sandy Hook, Lot G, is different. It's easy to find and it is the first stretch of federal shore where what the National Park Service calls a "clothing-optional lifestyle" is tolerated.

It's sort of a "don't-ask-don't-tell" situation, since no Park Service literature refers to the sanctioned nudism. If you have a close encounter of the fourth kind, the usual exchange is:

"Uh, hello."

"Hi."

The naturists at Sandy Hook publish a newsletter called The Gunnison Gazette, which is distributed free upon request. They call themselves the Sandy Hook Suns.

The strangeness of Sandy Hook is not the nudism itself, but the fact that we textiles, while welcomed to mingle, are considered the weirdos.

Public Hangouts (1 of 5 pts)

There are no cafés or bars on Sandy Hook. However, let's give this place a point. After all, naturists, who are known for their secretive and private hangouts now have a public one.

Bizarre Geography (2 of 6 pts)

Sandy Hook looks somewhat like an upside-down Italy, sticking up from the Atlantic shore of New Jersey. It is visible from the coast of Brooklyn, New York, and from Sandy Hook you have a view of the Verrazano Narrows Bridge, the World Trade Towers and the old apartment buildings of Brighton Beach.

This is the bizarre situation of a place geographically isolated from civilization, yet with a view of the metropolis.

"Viewed on a clear day from the drawbridge off Route 36 in Sea Bright, this six-and-a-half-mile sandspit seems to extend north all the way to New York City." But viewed on the map, it looks as if Sandy Hook is giving the finger to New York.

Upended Facilities (2 of 3 pts)

The area's architecture dates back to the 1890s. Park Service personnel and families live in underinsulated officer row houses. Some of the row houses remain vacant while others are rented out to non-profit organizations for weekend retreats. These yellow brick Georgian Revival houses are accompanied by the spooky fortifications whose first sections were hastily built during the War of 1812, to be "modernized" in 1859. Beyond Fort Hancock is the 228-year old Sandy Hook Lighthouse, the oldest continuously functioning beacon in the U.S.

In an age of overdeveloped, streamlined coastlines, no one is likely to mistake Sandy Hook for a suburb.

Non-Mainstream Recreation (2 of 5 pts)

Sandy Hook is a two-shift place. During the first shift, there are the park personnel, four different educational institutions, the various civic and environmental groups that rent space, and the bathers and surfers (Surfer's Cove is Parking Lot C). It's a real community with a daytime population of about 1,000.

But then there's the predawn culture of striper anglers, fishing for striped bass. Stripers can grow to fifty or sixty pounds.

According to Ian Frazier, "striper anglers have big, gill-like necks, wear clothing in layers, and yawn ostenstatiously in daylight. They are famous for their divorce rate; the striper is a night creature, and its pursuers must be, too."

"People have caught many big stripers at Sandy Hook," adds Frazier, an angler himself. "It is among the prime striper-fishing grounds on the East Coast."

Freedom in the Bedroom (1 of 2 pts)

The State of New Jersey has comprehensive legislation against discrimination based on sexual orientation, but nudists are prudes when it comes to public sex acts and it's tough to find a private room on The Hook.

Depending on one's hour of arrival and departure, Sandy Hook can metamorphize from backcountry to urban; since there's only one way off the peninsula, the Hook even has a rush hour! The first stop for hungry drivers making their evening exodus is the village of Highlands, where you'll find an array of seafood restaurants from cheap to expensive.

TOTAL POINTS: 12

SANTA FE, NEW MEXICO

The artist, once wrote Charles Bukowski, is always sitting on the doorsteps of the rich. But what would happen if artists became the dominant culture of a whole city?

Santa Fe offers the rare case study where this has happened. According to *Fodor's 94 USA*, Santa Fe is the country's third most important art center, after New York and Los Angeles. This seems incongruous for a city with a population of only 56,000.

The problem begins when good people from around the nation,

usually from Los Angeles, discover the aesthetic qualities of Santa Fe, the pristine sky, the coarse textures of the surrounding mountains, the mellow adobe pastels of the hilly town and the living history of the Native Americans and Hispanics. According to Gloria Mendoza, a long-time activist for the poor in Santa Fe, as newcomers moved in, many Hispanic and Native American families moved out. In the Canyon Road area, art galleries began taking over houses, and many residents of the newly prosperous and sought-after neighborhood couldn't afford the steep real-estate taxes brought about by property reappraisals.

There may be no other place in the world with a combined natural and man-made setting as deeply beautiful as Santa Fe. Yet the incursion of aesthetically-minded people into this city ex-emplifies how good intentions can have imperialistic consequences.

Indeed, some members of the local power structure were in cahoots with the newcomers, as the city spent millions to attract developers, tourists, wealthy celebrities and retirees.

Ironically, as the arts burgeon, some local artists are concerned that operas and art galleries are eclipsing the beauty of the land and the cultural heritage of New Mexico.

Having feared that Santa Fe was well on its way to becoming a art theme park, I reluctantly considered excluding it from this book. But now the situation is turning around.

Independent Politics (2 of 3 pts)

As soon as Ms. Debbie Jaramillo was elected Mayor, city officials began discussing a moratorium on hotel construction. Things began happening on the Plaza, the center of town, where the Pueblo Indians display their jewelry and blanket crafts in the arcade. The Plaza is the site of public buildings, such as the Palace of the Governors, which have been in continuous use for more than four centuries.

Thousands of residents flooded this historic downtown, usually dominated by tourists, to celebrate "Take Back the Plaza Day."

The gathering became a weekly event known as Raza in the Plaza. "Raza" literally means race but it is used as a metaphor referring to the Chicano or Hispanic people from the U.S. Actually, people of all ethnic backgrounds participated in the protests.

Cross-Cultural (5 pts)

They were concerned that economic growth was destroying the ethnic diversity of the city's dynamic tri-cultural heritage of Hispanic, Native American and Anglo, which manifests itself as an assortment of congenial, diverse neighborhoods.

Unconventional Regional Customs (4 of 6 pts)

The local activists did not limit their protests to public gatherings. A no-growth movement has been particularly effective. Even the environmentalist magazine, *Outside*, had trouble getting permission to construct its new solar-powered headquarters at the base of the Sangre de Cristo Mountains.

Yet more ironic was the no-growthers' victory in preventing Shirley MacLaine from building a subdivision on the top of a mountain overlooking Santa Fe. MacLaine should have had support from the city's large population of new-agers.

According to a recent article in *Forbes Magazine*, Santa Fe "has become a healing mecca, particularly for pilgrims seeking...the latest in out-of-body care." The local Yellow Pages and newspapers abound with ads for counseling in the Shamanic arts, cranio-sacral therapy, in which the mind lets the body free to express "its knowingness," and events like the Psychic & Bodyworker Fair.

Pedestrian Friendly (4 pts)

Taos is "Santa Fe's funkier sibling," but Santa Fe itself has remained relatively free from modern blandness. If the city's seducing aromas, colors, textures, human oddities and earthen architecture don't get you out of your car and on to the street, the traffic will.

The only inhibiter of a good walk is the outdoor mallishness of certain boutique-ridden areas.

Alternative Economy (2 of 3 pts)

As a shopping alternative, there is Trader Jack's Santa Fe Flea Market, where "the vendors frequently are as entertaining as the merchandise." And, boutiques or no boutiques, the Pueblo Indians are still able to market their art and artisan work with minimal impact from the middleman.

Mixed-Use Zoning (4 pts)

While commerce may have a choking effect on certain streets, it has assured that the center of the city will not be divvied up into one-dimensional enclaves.

Public Hangouts (5 pts)

The Plaza itself is one place to try stopping time in its tracks. With antiquity still alive in this setting, who knows, at least, from a plaza bench, we have a chance of slowing down the process of psychological time.

While Santa Fe is a shoppers' paradise, it is also a fine place to choose a café or restaurant, sip a coffee or a glass of red wine and watch other people shop.

Away from the upscale shopping areas are numerous neighborhood haunts where one can savor a brew and soak in the atmosphere of the Southwest.

Positive-Expectation Gambling (1 of 2 pts)

The New Mexican racing circuit spends part of its season in Santa Fe, with bottom-of-the barrel races for horses that have no chance to make it in the big time.

With seven progressives on the eight-member city council, there is a trend toward involving the residents in economic decision-making. Santa Fe will never again be a best-kept secret, but it is moving in a direction that will preserve the city's exceptional tricultural ambience.

Founded in 1609, Santa Fe is the second oldest city in the USA, after St. Augustine, Florida. The Pueblo Indians in the towns surrounding Santa Fe trace their heritage back 2,000 years. Hopefully, the new wave of benevolent colonizers will not do to Santa Fe what the conquerors of the West could never do.

For visitors' information, call 800/777-2489.

TOTAL POINTS: 27

SEASIDE, FLORIDA

Can you plan an offbeat place or must it just happen? A team of visionary developers and architects got together at the beginning of the last decade in order to counteract the dehumanizing trends of suburbia and automobile-dominated lifestyles. The result was a planned community on the Florida Panhandle. They managed to stick this place on the edge of the sea, but by resorting to utopian planning, did they force the issue? When do planned Main Street good-old days became so self-conscious that they mock themselves?

Unconventional Regional Customs (2 of 6 pts)

Sea coasts everywhere are vulnerable to the condominium syndrome. A stroll beneath the typical row of coastal highrises and colorless developments can be an insulting experience to one who expects the ocean to be respected. Even more offensive is the separation of commerce and residence, obligating human beings to use a machine to get from one parking lot to another for every loaf of bread and quart of milk, a process that is hardly in tempo with the romance of the sea.

With their plans and actions, the developers of Seaside were swimming against the thirty-year current of suburban wastelands.

Much of their efforts were directed toward avoiding the sensory deprivation that characterizes typical suburbia. These include reddish concrete pavement, pink, yellow and aqua pastel house facades, and sandy, fenced foot paths cutting through the middle of blocks, so uncomfortably close to windows that one resident labeled it the "voyeur system."

Most observers think that this ambitious project has been an artistic success. Writer Philip Langdon calls the streets of Seaside "visual knockouts."

Mixed-Use Zoning and Layout (4 pts)

In the spirit of traditional towns, Seaside purposely mixes shops, public buildings and dwellings of various sizes. The commercial, the public and the private are all linked by a network of convivial streets.

Pedestrian Friendly (4 pts)

The streets are narrow, no more than 18 feet wide, so that pedestrians have the advantage over cars.

Property owners were encouraged to invent the style of their own fence, so that no two fences on the block would be alike. Required front porches must be near enough to the street so that people on the porch can have a conversation with passersby without raising their voices.

Meanwhile, no street stretches infinitely to the horizon, except the main road, so that the eye is never left gazing upon nothing or nowhere.

On evenings, streets are used as promenades, while during the day, people can walk to the tiny, classical post office, the wooden Sip & Dip refreshment stand, Bud & Alley's seafood restaurant and an array of stores and shops.

Public Hangouts (2 of 5 pts)

The architects argue that streets should be like public rooms, "places that are pleasurable to occupy and that invite human interchange": the exact opposite of modern suburbia.

"In recent decades," Langdon writes, "Americans have been focusing too much on the house itself and too little on the neighborhood, too much on interior luxury and too little on public amenity." Seaside reverses the trend, designed with the intimacy of a European village.

For their vision, the planners of this community have won awards. One writer called the place "a visual stunner." *Time Magazine* referred to it as a "down home utopia." And despite the place's fame, it conserves its slow-pace lifestyle.

With its art galleries and Mediterranean-style open market, as well as its eclectic schedule of events and wine-music festivals, it seems too perfect.

Mike Sinclair, author of *The Rough Guide* for Florida (1993), thinks it is indeed too perfect. He calls the cottages "pseudo-Victorian," and the pastel paintwork "silly." Of the red brick streets he complains: "it seems antisocial to leave so much as a footprint." The place is too expensive and exclusive for him to ever feel a part of it.

He recommends as an "antidote to Seaside's sterility" the town of Grayton, a few miles down Route 30A. A number of artists have been attracted to that place's ramshackle wooden dwellings and now reside there. Grayton has a beachside gallery as well as the open-air workshops of wood sculptor Joe Elmore, whose artistic tool is a chainsaw.

I'm not as ready as Sinclair to give up on Seaside. Maybe a few hoboes will show up one day and pitch a tent, somebody's teenage kids will begin a rock band and the town will generally loosen up. Remember, it was intended to take the place of a resort or suburb so it should be compared with those types of places.

It reminds me of the poetry of André Breton, the theoretical founder of surrealism in literature. That movement preached total freedom. But abstract theory and concrete freedom contradict each other. Breton's poems seemed too planned. Nevertheless he was responsible for liberating a large contingent of followers and since Breton, poetry has never been the same.

For the time being, we won't get involved in the polemics. Someone had to start somewhere to reverse the tide of sensory deprivation in the bleak landscapes of modern housing developments. Architects and town planners Andres Duany and Elizabeth Plater-Zyberk have begun to turn it around.

TOTAL POINTS: 12

TAKOMA PARK, MARYLAND

Takoma Park is a rather unassuming town where front porches have stood firm against the back-deck invasion and old houses on commercially valuable terrain have diverted the developers' wrecking instincts by opening their doors to commerce.

When Pizza Hut wanted to move into town, it looked as if the first step in the corporate invasion would set off a chain reaction leading Takoma Park into the era of minimalls and parking lots. But the citizens' associations put up their invisible moat and Pizza Hut could not break through.

Unconventional Regional Customs (4 of 6 pts)

As more than a symbolic gesture to the varied cultures of its residents, Takoma Park permits non-citizens to vote in municipal elections. It has declared itself a nuclear-free zone and a sanctuary city for political refugees. The city has a unique tool-lending library, a smart investment for fixing up the neighborhood. Holistic health care seems to dominate over the mainstream variety.

In this urban village, community activism is the rule rather than the exception. One television reporter referred to Takoma Park as "a kooky laboratory for radical ideas."

Cross-Cultural (4 of 5 pts)

To some extent the various cultures, from Latin America, Africa and Asia, maintain their own identities, independent of the white population, but there are a number of activities in which they join together, whether it be for the annual folk and street fairs or to work on community issues. The downtown survives without any major chain stores. There is a Middle Eastern food store, an African cultural center, a metaphysical chapel, and a craft-import store.

Indeed, the cross-cultural persuasion is also a cross-national identity, with many of the locals holding on to deep ties with far-flung nations. We met several Takoma Park residents who are ex-Peace Corps volunteers.

Public Hangouts (1 of 5 pts)

Although the town is not lined with cafés, there are several inviting eateries, including bakery-cafés, ethnic restaurants and jazz clubs, all of which offer alternative atmospheres and are conducive to eating and drinking slowly to the accompaniment of chatting with neighbors.

Pedestrian Friendly (4 pts)

Once out on the streets, a stroll is as delightful for the eyes as it is good for the body. A "trompe l'oeil" mural sits above the Takoma Woman's Center and another one is found down the road across from the fire station.

The Metro to Washington, D.C. is within walking distance, meaning that theoretically a person who lives in Takoma Park and works in D.C. could survive without an automobile.

A municipal parking lot is found in the rear of the commercial center so that one walks by storefronts instead of parking lots. The preservation of old architecture adds joy to the walk.

Upended Facilities (1 of 3 pts)

Several commercial establishments are maintained in buildings that used to be homes. Incredibly, the tudor mansion that houses an auto mechanic shop was originally built as a filling station/garage.

Mixed-Use Zoning (1 of 4 points)

People reside within the downtown district or within a short walk of it. Technically the zoning laws are not mixed use, but the boundary between commercial and residential districts is blurred by exceptions to the zoning, including a multidwelling apartment building that was there before the zoning laws were passed.

The city spills over into Washington, D.C., so that what looks and feels like Takoma Park has a split personality.

Alternative Economy (1 pts out of 3)

Street vending is not a custom beyond the local fairs, but a colorful farmers market shows up every Sunday from 10:00-2:00 from April through Thanksgiving. The folk fair and the street festival are two annual weekends when ma and pa can hustle their wares.

Independent Politics (3 pts)

Takoma Park has maintained its character largely because of its activist community and a responsive municipal government. While other nearby Maryland communities were making major concessions to developers and their demolition teams, Takoma Park was defending its right to be different.

Recently, citizens' groups, wearied from fighting off Pizza Hut and other incursions, are demanding that municipal officials become more proactive in defending the integrity of the city.

These officials are non-partisan in their politics.

The local populace has what can be considered a third-world consciousness, as exemplified by the presence of Arawak Books, billed as a Caribbean/Third World book store.

Positive-Expectation Gambling (2 pts)

Laurel Race Course, with live racing as well as a large menu of simulcast races from other major tracks, is only eight miles down the road.

Freedom in the Bedroom (2 pts)

Montgomery County, Maryland, has passed comprehensive legislation barring discrimination based on sexual orientation.

Takoma Park is dead serious about defending the rights of the disenfranchised, but at night, it knows how to have a good time. Taliano's, for example, is an animated jazz restaurant. One of the best jazz clubs in the mid-Atlantic region is Takoma Station Tavern. Unlike other clubs, whose late hours thwart the attendance of parents and working people, Takoma Station bends the rules of jazz tradition and offers music during happy hours Thursdays and Fridays, with a Saturday "Art Meets Jazz" program from noon to 6pm. The food is priced very reasonably for a spot of this stature.

While nearby Chevy Case and Bethesda are very conscious of their beauty and wealth, Takoma Park remains a bit unmanicured. But don't let that fool you. For 21 years, House-and-Garden Tours have opened local residences to the public. The Community Improvement Board makes sure that those who cannot afford to keep up their property receive economic help.

A dynamic Youth Outreach Program has counselors who go out to difficult corners and invite youths to participate in various activities, including a Midnight Basketball League. The program sponsors a lawn service that provides temporary jobs, such as gardening and moving, to youths who need income.

According to one long-time resident, "a number of kids that were headed in the wrong direction did a complete turnaround thanks to the program. Some even return after graduating college to coach in the program."

TOTAL POINTS: 23

TAOS, NEW MEXICO

In Taos, New Mexico, the land itself is a major protagonist in human creation. There is scarcely a distinction between the structures of art and architecture and the formations and textures of geography.

Bizarre Geography (4 of 6 pts)
New Mexico provides a dramatic setting for adventures and lifestyles that defy the conventions of American culture. First, there is the dynamic physical setting, whose contrasts assure a variety of sensorial experiences.

Six of the continent's seven biological life zones are found within the state's borders, ranging down from the cold and windy arctic-alpine country above the timberline to the often torrid lower Sonoran desert. Taos is within striking distance of most of these variations.

One is served by these extremes in a palatable way, for the dry air moderates the summer heat while the almost constant sunlight warms the winters.

Near Taos, sudden summer snowstorms are not unknown in the mountain roads above the town.

Cross-Cultural (5 pts)

Along with geographic diversity comes a dynamic cultural mix. Native American cultures, Hispanic and Angloamericans meet here in a unique configuration. The 19 Pueblo tribes believed that people were part of nature. Their quest for harmony minimized personal ambition and material acquisition. This peaceful outlook absorbed the warrior cultures that invaded their territory.

The more gold-hungry of the Spanish conquistadores and later Anglo-Americans sought their fortunes elsewhere. As a result, the Pueblo Indians received the more tolerant, or at least, less frantic incursions of outsiders. Clearly, the Anglos became the dominant of the three groups, but the unique configuration of these cultures has allowed for relative peaceful coexistence and interaction.

Unconventional Regional Customs (5 of 6 pts)

The Pueblo Indians are amongst the most conservative of Native American groups. Here, conservative means faithful to traditional lifestyles and philosphies. An outward manifestation is the shunning of electricity and plumbing. More consequential is the communal use of land. The Pueblos managed a successful revolt in 1680 that insured the succession of their culture.

Meanwhile, many Hispanics maintain a world view that allows for survival of magical realism, a perspective typical of some novels of John Nichols. For example, there are still "curanderos" who use centuries-old medical treatments. More inwardly, there remains a respect for the supernatural. The charm of the Hispanics is bittersweet, since they have been victimized by the power structure and the harsh land.

Within this context of geographic and cultural diversity, Taos steps up along with Paris and New York as an art capital of the world. This is not to say that arts are inherently an unconventional lifestyle. But Taos is one of few places in the U.S. where art becomes THE dominant lifestyle. More than ten percent of its residents are painters, sculptors, writers, musicians or art entrepreneurs.

In reality, there are three nearby spots within the same Taos jurisdiction. The principal community or downtown is predominantly Hispanic. Here lies the touring base for the surrounding area.

Three miles to the northeast is Taos Pueblo, where the Tiwa language survives. The Taos Pueblo has been the home of the Tiwas for more than 900 years. Two massive adobe buildings, the world's first high-rise apartments, have not changed much since they were first observed by the Spaniards 450 years ago. Made of earth itself, the buildings blend with the land around them.

Finally, there is Ranchos de Taos, a small community four miles south of Taos center, nestled around the magnificent but mellow Saint Francis de Asis Church-Sculpture, the one with no windows that many of us have already seen in works by Georgia O'Keeffe and Ansel Adams.

Pedestrian Friendly (3 of 4 pts)

The best way to see Taos is on foot. The main strip is often a slow bumper-to-bumper progression of cars, with pedestrians in the passing lane. Free municipal parking as well as inexpensive commercial lots are mercifully out of view but handy to the visitor who wishes to experience the town on foot.

The automobile is needed, however, to explore the region.

Public Hangouts (4 of 5 pts)

Streets here are often winding lanes lined with traditional adobe homes, many of them over a hundred years old. An abundance of galleries and cultural centers, all with the typical adobe design, are within walking distance of each other.

The hangout most receptive to alternative life styles is the Mainstreet Bakery, less than two blocks from the plaza. Vegetarian and natural food is served, mainly breakfast, lunch and snacks, at inexpensive prices. There is a large selection of publications that support counterculture ways of living.

Local New Mexican cuisine can be found at Roberto's Restaurant. Housed in an adobe building over 160 years old, each intimate dining room has high ceilings, hardwood floors, no more than five tables and a fireplace. Inexpensive.

Cafés offer outdoor seating during the summer, including Dori's Bakery & Café and the Bent Street Deli & Café.

If you prefer upscale places, Taos has a variety of options. The town's animated bookstores contribute to a Left Bank Parisian ambience.

The Adobe Bar presents an unpredictable program of music. It's not a niche place. So on Wednesdays and Sundays between 6:00 and 9:00, you may get jazz, classical, folk, Hispanic and who knows what else? There's no cover charge.

The intimacy of the street scene is derived from both the content within the gathering places and their form; since adobe architecture comes directly out of the earth, one cannot separate nature from the man-made. The result is a sense of unity.

Alternative Economy (2 of 3 pts)

Street life is enhanced during the Taos Spring Art Festival (three weeks, end of May through June) and the Taos Fall Art Festival (end of September into beginning of October). Perhaps no other town in the world spends a full eighth of the year presenting arts festivals. Local craftspeople thus have an incoming market for their goods and the playing field is tilted in favor of family businesses over corporations.

Mixed-Use Zoning (4 pts)

The layout of Taos has been determined by the centuries of its existence, by the land, and by the mix of cultures in the region, not by city or regional planners.

Non-Mainstream Entertainment (1 of 5 pts)

The Taos Pueblo Pow Wow is a dance competition and parade drawing tribes from throughout North America, held on the weekend after July 4. There are other seasonal festivals that include Native American dancing. Years ago, I attended a pow wow in which the visitors were welcomed to dance. While the imagery of that experience is now rather vague, I still feel the voices rising and falling like the wail of sax in the higher registers, the shuffle-like rhythms, and the warmth of a converging community.

The seductive mountain country around Taos celebrates a variety of side trips of cultural and natural interest. In fact, every direction out of town leads to one revelation or another. One trip of interest follows Route 64, 10 miles west of Taos, where the Rio Grande Gorge Bridge crosses 650 feet above the canyon. Be Monet for an afternoon and you'll see the colors of the cliff walls change as the day eases by.

Continuing on Route 64 for about 55 miles, you'll arrive at Tierra Amarilla. Here is the scene of a major rebellion in 1967. I interviewed the leader of this rebellion, Reies Tijerina, following his release from prison. His group, called the Alianza, led an armed raid on the Tierra Amarilla courthouse. The object was to stake a claim, based on original Land Grants that proved that the area's Hispanic residents were the true proprietors of the land. The Alianza cited the Treaty of Guadalupe-Hidalgo (1848), which declared that original Land Grants would be respected in territory won by the U.S. from Mexico.

During the raid, three law officers were wounded while a deputy sheriff and newspaper reporter were abducted. Tijerina went to jail as a result. Although the Alianza received much nationwide support, the movement died down and there was no change in the land system of Tierra Amarilla.

Today, the people of Tierra Amarilla are attempting to maintain a 200-year old tradition of shepherding, spinning, weaving and dyeing. Tierra Wools (505/588-7231) sells clothing and blankets that result from this tradition.

In reality, the whole region surrounding Taos is a visual, cultural, historical and geographic feast. My goal is to one day hike through the area from town to town.

TOTAL POINTS: 28

UPC?UNTRY/PAIA, MAUI, HAWAII

This is one spectacular area of Hawaii where small towns have fought off the incursion of condominiums, and there is more to the local economy than tourism.

With the corporate economy under control, the cost of being here is moderate. Art and life are one. For art galleries, there is Manhattan, Paris, Taos/Santa Fe and Maui.

There are seven climactic zones, from tropical rain forests to cool mountains, all accessible by bicycle. If you don't like pedaling, start at the top, 10,000 feet above sea level!

The Makawao-Paia corridor of Maui contains the greatest geographic diversity within the smallest area. It has a counter-culture atmosphere, and is strategically located between the traditional but voluptuous town of Hana to the east and Kapalua Beach to the west, where the mountains come down to the sea.

Non-Mainstream Entertainment/Recreation (5 pts)

The weirdest thing about Maui's entertainment is that so much of it is for free. With all the hype about Hawaii as a tourist center, one would have expected a paucity of low-budget outings.

Maui for free includes festivals around the calendar, walking maps for the Maui Experimental Agricultural Garden, at Kula, self-guided maps for the historic walk around Lahaina, the Hana Cultural Center, and hiking maps from the Hawaii Nature Center, RR1, Box 518, Wailuku, Maui, HI 96793 (808/244-6500).

Hiking may seem like a mainstream activity, but when accomplished in the crater of a volcano, in this case Haleakala, it takes on a bizarre twist. Whale watching is hardly an unusual activity; but Maui whale watching, by waters declared a "cetacean sanctuary," includes the mating season, with these gentle giants uninhibited in their erotic leaps and spouts...a must for kinky voyeurs. Approximately 1,500 whales winter in Maui waters. Babies weigh 2,000 pounds at birth.

Snorkeling is another more-or-less common activity; but how about snorkeling in a submerged volcano crater at Molokini? Because of the contours of the crater, you'll feel as if you were in an aquarium. While surfing exists in many places, Mokuleia Beach may be the greatest of all tests; no wonder it's called "Slaughterhouse."

More free attractions include the Lahaina Jodo Mission, with the largest Buddha outside Asia, and the Maui Tropical Plantation at Waikapu.

Finally, there is the Friday "Art Night" at the Lahaina Gallery, where complimentary wine and hors d'oeuvres are accompanied by music.

Unconventional Regional Customs (4 of 6 pts)

In Hawaii the word "mana," the spiritual presence that inspires art, is attributed to Maui itself. For many in Maui, art and life are one.

Various businesses fit into this extended definition of art. For example, you can visit the M. Uradomo Farms, where they grow the famous Maui onion, so sweet it can almost be eaten like an apple (808/878-1828).

Hippies survive in Paia, but our sources don't agree as to how they make their living, suggesting extremes from "independently wealthy" to "trading and bartering."

The ancient Hawaiians, aware that resources were finite, established an elaborate system of "kapu" (taboo) laws regulating the human impact on nature. Many modern laws are based on that sacred premise. A series of greenbelts, closed to all motorized traffic, provide low-impact access to stretches of coastline and other natural wonders. Bikeways cross the whole island.

While the hula is already overpublicized, it rates being included here because it was once banned for what New England missionary C.S. Stewart wrote: "exhibitions of unrivaled licentiousness and abominations which must forever remain untold."

Cross-Cultural (5 pts)

Makawao and neighboring towns have the art gallery crowd side by side with the cowboy-&-grain store culture. At Paia, the surfer culture mingles with the arts crowd and the hippies, with a Buddhist mission overlooking the proceedings; all of Maui is referred to as "Chop Suey" because of its racial diversity and combinations of East and West: Hawaiian, Chinese, Korean, Filipino, Portuguese and German. Various cultures celebrate each others' festivals.

Bizarre Geography (6 pts plus 2 bonus pts)

From the Haleakala Volcano summit to the beach at Paia Bay, the elevation drops 10,000 feet in 38 miles! Guided downhill bike tours cut through flower farms, cowboy ranches and the small towns of Upcountry, to the beach at Paia. The record low temperature for Hawaii is at Haleakala, 14 degrees centigrade, January 2, 1961. Meanwhile, the highest recorded temperature in Maiu is lower than comparable stats for any other state of the U.S., even Alaska!

Catch the scent of wild ginger on 52 hairpin turns on the road to Hana (including 56 one-lane bridges). "Spectacular," is an understatement; compare this to a straight-and-flat trip across Kansas or Texas. Compare the white, gold, salt-and-pepper, green or garnet beach sands, volcanic in origin, to the more mudane sands along the Atlantic coast. Of the 81 Maui beaches, 39 do not have public facilities, allowing for the alternatives of solitude or lively crowds.

Seven climactic zones on one island! The second highest waterfall in the United States! Parts of West Maui are so rugged they have never been explored! On the west coast is Kahakuloa Head, sixty stories of wind-sculpted rock that looks like a lonely coast of Ireland. At Nakalele Point, giant geysers.

When assigning the point total for this category, we faced a dilemma. The six points maximum didn't fit. On the one hand, we could have deducted a point or two because of geographic overkill. So much beauty might kill the senses. On the other hand, it was not one type of beauty; there are all kinds of bizarre geographic aberrations. Six points was not enough. So Maui earns two bonus points. All superlatives become understatements when referring to this island's startling imagery.

Mixed-Use Zoning (2 of 4 pts)

From Makawao to Paia, small-town atmosphere has managed to stave off the incursion of modern blandness, family businesses have outfinessed corporate chains, and one is more likely to find places that feature a mingling of commercial and residential functions.

Alternative Economy (2 of 3 pts)

With this void in the corporate economy, ma-and-pa businesses and local crafts and art producers have a market for their goods.

Pedestrian Friendly (2 of 4 pts)

Economic alternatives inject life into streets. Although one needs a car on the island and you can't hop on a metro to go from place to place, a person can survive as a pedestrian by resorting to the bicycle as the primary means of transportation when not on foot. The Maui government has gone to great lengths to provide paths and amenities for cyclists' independence.

Public Hangouts (3 of 5 pts)

Each beach has its own type of crowd. The beaches themselves are the consummate hangout. A few beaches are either clothing optional or tolerate discreet nudity.

Some restaurants qualify as bonafide hangouts. Tom, Maui resident and refugee from Cleveland, recommends Pollies (in Makawao), for its atmosphere and Mexican food. Pollies offers outdoor seating.

Across the road from Pollies, Casanova's family Italian restaurant gets points from Tom because visitors may select small portions if they have come more for social reasons than out of hunger.

In Paia, he recommends the German food at Wunderbar Café Restaurant, with outdoor patio seating adding spice to the atmosphere. The Paia Fish Market is an informal walk-up place, but the food is well worth it.

For free information on everything about Maui, including lodging, contact the Maui Visitors Bureau: 808/244-3530.

TOTAL POINTS: 31

VENICE, CALIFORNIA

If you are an odd person, you will feel right at home in Venice, just like Harry Perry, the guy who plays his portable electric guitar while he rollerskates in and out of boardwalkers. Showing off one's weirdness is the way to fit in with this community. Venice is the world capital of exhibitionism.

Unconventional Regional Customs (6 pts)

My daughter Siomara hangs out in Venice. These are some of the people she has seen on a regular basis.

"A very skinny, unhealthy looking man with a giant sign: MEAT IS MURDER. He shows graphic pictures of slaughtered cows and warns passersby against eating meat.

"A guy with no legs and no arms but one finger coming out of the arm stub who dances on his leg stubs, using a chair to balance, with back-up music, either a marraca player or a radio...he gets good donations.

"A guy wrapped in snakes.

"A man who has been on the Arsenio Hall program who coerces people to watch his show and to dance. He picks people of different ethnic backgrounds and plays music he thinks they'll dance to."

Other sightings around the Venice boardwalk, which is really a cement sidewalk, are:

Tarahumara Indians dressed in feather headdresses and silver loincloths doing a sunworship dance...

Rollerbladers doing pirouettes and other stunts...

A juggler tossing chainsaws...

A hillbilly yodeler, in knee-torn overalls, balancing upside down between two dinette chairs...

A woman in gold platform shoes and a red wig acting out a routine as a rotating human statue...

And of course, the narcissistic body builders at Muscle Beach.

In this context of exhibitionism, other customs normally considered on the fringe of the mainstream hardly seem offbeat: poetry readings at Beyond Baroque, Christmas boat races, meditation classes at Ordinary Dharma and roller blades and bicycles replacing the automobile as the primary mode of transportation.

A number of Venice acts have become famous and yet still return to their roots. Example: Bad Boyz, three African Americans and a Colombian, who do adagio skating, with jazz and hip-hop footwork and acrobatics, and Barry "the Lion" Gordon, the stride pianist of the streets, playing in the style of Art Tatum, identified by his goatee and high hat.

 ## Pedestrian Friendly (4 pts)

With its street and beach life, Venice is the epitome of a pedestrian friendly place, if you don't get hit by roller bladers. The human spectacle is only part of the animated setting. Venice, along with neighboring Santa Monica, is an open canvas for street muralists. The creative energy of so many Venice artists comes alive on street corners and storefronts, in alleys and alongside roadways.

Among the murals are several "trompe l'oeil" works of art, the kind where you think a person is looking out of a second floor window only to discover the third time you see it that it is only a painting.

An example of the Venice mural imagination, near the beach, is "Venus Rising from the Foam," a parody of Botticelli depicting the goddess of love on roller skates.

Relatively cool in the summer but mild in the winter, thanks to a benign ocean current, no place in the world can rival Venice as a haven for confirmed peripatetics.

Even in more residential areas, no stroll in Venice is mundane. The streets were designed by Europhile Abbot Kinney at the turn of the century to mimic Italy's city of canals. Along California Venice's canals are rows of small cottage residences with narrow pedestrian walkways between them.

Reputed gang activity at night mutes some of the joy one may feel for the street life, but my friend Rick, a long time Venice resident, believes that his city is no more dangerous than anywhere else. "You've got to mind your Ps and Qs wherever you are," he

said. "I'm not saying you wouldn't read about it and think there's a problem. People come from all over for the beach. That means that conceivably two guys from rival gangs could cross each other's path. But I love Venice and I'm not going anywhere else."

Cross-Cultural (5 pts)

All races, classes and economic sectors of the population come to mingle in Venice. A stubborn middle class has not fled to safer places, preferring Venice's hot-sauce flavor over the blandness of quieter neighborhoods. This phenomenon stabilizes the community.

A magnet school for international languages, various multi-ethnic community groups and a seemingly infinite parade of international and ethnic restaurants are all part of the Venice mosaic.

Public Hangouts (5 pts)

Venice is the embodiment of a public place. The whole town functions like an extension of one's home or a community front porch. Everyone in Venice has staked out a favorite hangout: cafés, benches near the boardwalk, the boardwalk itself, bars, the beach.

One element that makes Venice distinct in this realm: it is very much a moving hangout. Social interaction often takes place on bicycles and roller skates.

Alternative Economy (3 pts)

Street vending is lifted to the level of an art form in this town. For example, there is a hemp stand, the plant from which marijuana is derived. In the booth, information is displayed about marijuana. You can buy a Bible printed on hemp paper, jewelry and clothing made from hemp, medicine derived from hemp. Bumper sticker: "My other car was seized by the DEA."

Oh, how the underground economy has progressed. Another friend from Venice, Gene, reports that on a street corner where they used to sell drugs, someone walked up to him and whispered, "Computers ...computers for sale...lowest prices in town."

Back above ground, a farmers market has become a major institution on the streets of Venice.

Positive-Expectation Gambling (2 pts)

Hollywood Park race track in nearby Inglewood cards top-level racing and simulcasting in the off season, and includes a poker room. "Who needs to go to Las Vegas anymore?" Rick says. "We have all the positive games right here!"

Bizarre Geography (2 of 6 pts)

Other cities at the same lattitude, some not far inland from Venice, suffer unbearable summers, but this Pacific village receives the Japan Current that keeps it mild all year. The nearby Pacific Palisades and Santa Monica Mountains save the coastline from the symmetry and flatness of other beaches. Venice's canals may have begun as a tacky idea, but they remain to alleviate strollers from the typical street-buildings-street-buildings urbanscape.

Non-Mainstream Recreation (6 pts)

Enjoying the Venice streets is, of course, the primary form of entertainment, but not the only one.

Beach volleyball was born here, and eclipses lesser sports, such as football and baseball.

The Venice Art Walk raises funds to help the Venice Family Clinic, a mainstay in providing good health care for low-income people. This annual spring Art Walk is unique because it breaks down conventional barriers between private and public. Volunteer homeowners open their living rooms to display private art collections to the public. Art lovers go house hopping in search of surprises. (If you're out to buy, the Art Walk also includes a silent auction.)

Independent Politics (2 of 3 pts)

Venice is the gathering place of a number of independent activist groups and community-based organizations that are beholden to neither Democrats nor Republicans.

Freedom in the Bedroom (2 pts)

The County of Los Angeles, including Venice, has a comprehensive law barring discrimination based on sexual orientation.

Unusual eating places abound. Our contacts recommend Miami Spice, a Cuban restaurant on Lincoln Blvd. My personal experience with Mexican eateries in Venice says the cheaper the facade, the more authentic the food.

TOTAL POINTS: 37

WARD, COLORADO

The unchlorinated Rocky Mountain water is so fresh and clean in Ward, Colorado, 22 miles west-northwest of Boulder and 9,253 feet above sea level, that the inhabitants don't want to waste it on things like flushing toilets.

Unconventional Regional Customs (6 pts)
Upholding this ideology is a Ward ordinance requiring outhouses instead of bathrooms, using a closed vault system.

"In Ward," Celeste says, "we still do things the old mountain way."

Boulder itself is no ordinary city. But the Boulder folks I interviewed look at Ward and nearby Gold Hill as the real non-conformist places.

"They're an eclectic group of people to say the least," said one Boulder woman. "We sense that Ward residents float about a mile higher than the town is actually elevated."

Ward was a ghost town in the late 60's, with only seven residents. Then hippies from all over the States moved in, seduced by the peace and quiet.

"How did they hear about the town?" I asked Celeste.

"It's a magical place. You're passing through and you want to stay."

The town's idealism implied by the "floating" metaphor has been brought down to earth by a nuts-and-bolts political system based on the town meeting.

Independent Politics (3 pts)
Unlike other towns in Boulder County, Ward is a self-rule municipality. Laws are made consensus style through a utopian general assembly. The whole town participates.

Mixed-Use Zoning (2 of 4 pts)
The town has decided against any type of zoning laws. As a consequence, residence and commerce are not segregated into different sectors. Of course, this is easier to do in a small town such as Ward than it would be in Boulder or Denver, so it is virtually a de facto accomplishment.

Visually, Ward has a captivating rough-hewn look to it, thanks to its mainly weatherbeaten structures.

"Most houses were built by out-of-work miners," says Celeste. "My house was built in 1855."

Public Hangouts (2 of 5 pts)

People hang out in Ward's general store, which sets aside a little area with seating for folks who want to stay and chat. The Millside Inn, just outside of town, is a comfortable restaurant, not known for its gourmet cooking, and there is also a resurrected town park.

Another restaurant in town had to close down when its owners had trouble fitting in with the town's community spirit.

The public consciousness of Ward's citizens extends beyond the physical structures that act as gathering places.

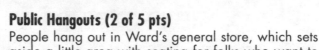

Bizarre Geography (2 of 6 pts)

The warmth of Ward residents helps to make up for the prolonged chill of what can become an eight-month winter. Twisting canyons and spectacular views make Ward the destiny of mountain bikers, "one of the more beautiful near-ghost towns in the state."

Ward is located on Highway 72, known as the Peak to Peak Highway. When covered with a smooth coat of snow, this is one of the more erotic landscapes in the country.

Also west of Boulder is the town of Gold Hill, often mentioned in the same breath with Ward. Although some Ward residents see Gold Hill as "more private and a little bit uppity," that town is also a refuge for counterculture types.

Lumping both alternative towns together, we now have a new region called WOBO, or "West Of Boulder."

I have been in places where it was necessary to use an outhouse in the winter. Needless to say, reading by the toilet was not the local custom. I asked Celeste whether Ward residents had heating in their outhouses.

"Some do and some don't. Some of us are tougher than others."

TOTAL POINTS: 15

WEST BERKELEY, CALIFORNIA

Artists, punk musicians, craftspeople, starving actors and others with an anarchist spirit have been moving to low-rent districts where they can practice their subsistence livelihoods without being forced to earn a large income in order to pay the rent. Typically, these pioneers have occupied old factories and warehouses, refurbishing them into living/working areas, usually without their measuring up to the building code.

Once the vanguard has made the neighborhood an interesting place, developers and commercial interests move in, gentrification takes place, and the original neighborhood innovators are priced out of the place they've given life to and transformed.

Threatened with a similar fate, residents of Berkeley's former M-Zone (M stands for "mixed") organized and negotiated with the developers and lobbied for local ordinances. They came out of the negotiations with a new Master Plan that institutionalized the mixed-use nature of their neighborhood. As a result, the supply of affordable housing has not vanished, and it looks as if the neighborhood will keep its character.

Without getting into too much detail, this revolutionary legal coup is worth explaining, since other progressive places have been groping for a way to protect their diversity and character once they are discovered by developers.

When the state legislature passed a law superseding West Berkeley ordinances that were supposed to protect the less fortunate, the community came up with alternatives. For example, the clever "arts and crafts ordinance" protects space for artists by square footage. If one artist moves out, the space must be rented to another artist. This tends to keep the rent down, as there aren't enough wealthy artists around to upset the dynamics.

With blue collar jobs declining and white collar jobs taking their place, especially in the biogenetics industry, the West Berkeley community came up with another creative bit of legislation. Certain areas were zoned only for heavy industry. Producers are only permitted to convert 25 percent of their facilities away from manufacturing.

Unconventional Regional Customs (6 pts)

These moves are bucking worldwide economic trends and their intention flies in the face of our property-driven culture. The community is purposely attempting to keep down the price of its property. If real estate taxes go up, the same diverse bunch of "pioneers" who made the neighborhood interesting would be priced out and forced to leave.

According to resident Mike Helm, this type of neighborhood contains many "people who are trying to live creative lives where they aren't having to work 60 hours a week to pay the rent." In other words, they are looking for the freedom to do what they like, and since what they like doesn't allow them to be in an upscale place, they settle for the space they can get.

There is an anarchist spirit that brings people here. A guy can't write the Great American Novel and work nine to five at the same time. He gives up the nine-to-five bit, and with it a middle-class lifestyle, in exchange for the precious commodity that characterizes this neighborhood: personal independence.

In other words, he gives up the American Dream in order to write the American Novel. Most people wouldn't make this trade. That's one reason why the people in the M-Zone are different.

"Just in the area where I live," Mike says, "there are people who have small woodworking shops in their houses, band rehearsal spaces, electronics shops. There's a car mechanic and three Koreans who run a restaurant on the corner...a greasy spoon."

Cross-Cultural (5 pts)

Drop into various West Berkeley hangouts and you'll see that the locals are of a wide variety of ethnic backgrounds. This is truly a multicultural community.

Rick, another local, explains that the neighborhood is made up of, in rough order of numbers, African Americans, whites, Latinos, Asians and Native Americans.

"The interaction between the groups is not the ideal we'd like it to be," Rick adds, "but at least you see clubs where the various groups show up."

The ordinances preventing high profit sectors from owning all the commercial space help keep the community diverse.

Public Hangouts (4 of 5 pts)

Brennan's Bar, the Home Café and Betty's Café are all spots where you can take your time, sip your brew slowly, chat with friends and neighbors and not be made to feel that you are overstaying your alloted time.

Brennan's, according to Mike, was originally a hotel for Chinese shrimp fishermen before becoming an Irish Pub.

Rick explains that there are both yuppie and working class hangouts scattered throughout the former M-Zone.

Alternative Economy (3 pts)

While street vending is not prevalent in West Berkeley, on nearby Telegraph Avenue, the streetscape comes alive with the underground economy.

Salvage operations allow people with low finances to participate in some form of economy that does not fit within the standardized definition of what people *should do*. Trading and bartering is possible thanks to these salvage businesses, the most famous known as Urban Ore.

The neighborhood also has a number of worker-owned collectives, such as the print shop called Ink Works.

An organic farm now adorns an industrial lot.

And thanks to the community ordinance, the neighborhood is still a friendly home for subsisting artists.

Bizarre Geographic (2 of 6 pts)

In this west end of Berkeley, you're right off the Bay. You can fish there without a license, and enjoy the unparalleled San Francisco Bay scenery. (Whether the

Bay is clean enough to harbor edible fish is another question.)

The climate is surprisingly benign, thanks to the right configuration of water currents. If you were at this latitude on the East Coast or in the Midwest, you'd have to deal with ice and snow in winter and unbearable heat and humidity in the summer, neither of which are a problem in Berkeley.

Mixed-Use Zoning (4 pts)

The whole concept of mixed-use zoning is defined by this part of town, although the rough edges of the industrial-residential dynamics have been softened in recent years.

Upended Facilities (3 pts)

Nevertheless, a large part of the neighborhood owes its existence to upended facilities, mainly factories and warehouses. The community has successfully managed to avert the Sohoization of its art colony.

Pedestrian Friendly (3 of 4 pts)

With its structural and human diversity, West Berkeley is an appealing place to be on foot. With a non-polluting electric shuttle slated to connect the neighborhood with the BART metro system, it will be possible to live without a car.

Further support in this direction comes from the active bicycle movement.

Positive-Expectation Gambling (2 pts)

In the next town up the road is Golden Gate Fields race track, which offers pari-mutuel wagering on live racing as well as simulcasts from other California tracks.

Freedom in the Bedroom (2 pts)

As could be expected from its history of tolerance, Berkeley, California has a comprehensive set of ordinances that bar discrimination based on sexual orientation.

According to Mike, "In the M-Zone, we basically see redevelopment as the equivalent of clear cutting the forest, then replacing it with even-aged trees that would be exactly the same height... Uneven-aged buildings, like an uneven-aged forest, make for a more vital neighborhood."

TOTAL POINTS: 34

YELLOW SPRINGS, OHIO

Yellow Springs has a good thing but it's not sure how to hold on to it. In a region of sleepy towns, this offbeat community is the nearest thing to utopia in the USA, brimming with idealists who know how to carry through on their ideals in practice.

But places evolve and the town cannot seem to decide which two forks in the road is the lesser of the two evils. On the one hand, there's a strong no-growth sentiment that would put a lid on the unaesthetic sprawl associated with commercial development. On the other hand, by successfully fending off shopping malls and fast food parking lots, the place becomes a magnet for folks seeking some spice in their lives. The resulting scarcity of space drives up property values, thus threatening to push out some sectors of the population that can no longer handle rising costs. With the push-out, Yellow Springs would lose some of the diversity it cherishes.

Cross-Cultural (2 of 5 pts)

Yellow Springs has the largest minority population of any town in the region, approximately 22 percent, mainly African Americans, blending with a strong international spirit. Both western and eastern religions are well-represented. International events and foreign films are frequently available. (While I was there, a film on Tibetan lamas was scheduled.) As one resident put it: "I have always imagined Yellow Springs like a loaf of six-grain bread among a shelf of white Wonder bread."

While there is plenty of commingling, the interaction between whites and blacks is not at the level most people would like it to be.

Unconventional Regional Customs (6 pts)

People seem to be collectively self-critical and the residents I spoke with say the town is nurturing its intercultural potential. With both intercultural relations and the no-growth-vs.-diversity dilemma, Yellow Springs is a town that questions itself in an ongoing manner, trying earnestly to avoid becoming a static object of history.

But this proactive stance against powerful trends doesn't fall into the trap of social engineering. There's a live-and-let-live attitude, and weirdness is an accepted trait. Some normally objective residents actually believe that a convergence of magnetic lines creates this positive energy, while others think it has to do with the spring water.

"A guy from Peru came here with an incurable illness and got cured," one woman told me. "He swears it's the town itself that made him well."

With its array of odd shops, Yellow Springs attracts people who are seeking an escape from chain-driven, corporate-dominated America.

"Do we want to become a tourist town?" is another current dilemma that the self-interrogating population is confronting.

Alternative Economy (3 pts)

With mainstream businesses largely absent from Yellow Springs, there's a void in the economy which is filled by all kinds of independent entrepreneurs. A women's co-op houses shops such as Fiber Fantasy, African Kijiji and Healing Arts. In this antithesis of a shopping mall I saw one saleslady doing her business barefooted, while in another shop, the owner's children were romping around.

On Xenia Avenue, the Route 68 main street, there's an art co-op, run by the artists themselves. No middlemen there. Even the greeting cards, for example, are hand made works of art.

At the Organic Grocery, I inquired about an alternative cancer medicine called shark cartilege, only to discover from the owner, a herbologist, that they don't carry the product because sharks are becoming an endangered species.

There's a real downtown movie house, The Little Art Theatre, whose offerings are much less predictable than the usual theatres. For one week you might get typical Hollywood films, only to find a zen fable for the next week.

Odd juxtapositions are the norm as the Yellow Springs News, a combination newspaper and humanist journal, has a vitamin distributor in its lobby.

At the Gemini Gallery of Music there are hand-crafted instruments and workshops on "the Healing Power of Music," involving improvising sessions in which no prior musical experience is necessary.

From late spring through autumn, Saturdays at 8:00 a.m., a farmers market comes into town. Along with the ten or twelve growers, small gardeners are allowed to participate. Produce must have been grown by the sellers themselves.

These are but a few examples of Yellow Springs' alternative enterprises.

Pedestrian Friendly (3 of 4 pts)

This alternative economy must be enjoyed on foot. Parking is right on the street, with no ugly lots in view. The streetscape invites you to abandon your car. Along with the eccentric shops and restaurants are an assortment of older buildings, blending European styles with mid-19th century America, and featuring Greek Revival.

A funky hangout called Ye Olde Trail Tavern & Restaurant is located in the first log home of Yellow Springs, built in 1827.

There are several T-junctions where the street runs into old brick buildings with Edward-Hopperesque cornices. An old-fashioned drugstore and a hardware store complete the anachronistic scene.

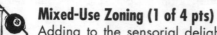

Mixed-Use Zoning (1 of 4 pts)

Adding to the sensorial delight of downtown is the fact that some people live there, with the rest of the town within walking distance. While many of the second floors on downtown streets have been converted to commercial use, second story residential apartments remain above a few storefronts.

Bizarre Geography (1 of 6 pts)

Although one can walk to the nearby gorge, it is more conveniently reached by automobile. The walk continues once you get there; within the area of the water-sculpted palisades are shaded hiking paths that keep it five or ten degrees cooler in summer. It is here that the much-touted Yellow Springs waters allegedly reinvigorate the body and soul.

Public Hangouts (3 of 5 pts)

Within the gorge there are two popular hangouts, called The Log and The Rock.

Various restaurants, cafés and bars, including Ye Olde Trail Tavern and the Dayton Street Gulch, are good slow-motion hangouts, along with a few well-placed street benches.

I found a few college kids on a Xenia Avenue bench. They revealed that their hangout in the gorge had been trashed by weekenders and that they had gone there to clean up the mess. One of them, a young woman who was born and raised in the town, made an observation that adds to the evidence for Yellow Springs passing the weirdness test.

"When I go other places," she said, "everyone else seems weird."

Upended Facilities (1 of 3)

Another feature of the stimulating ambience is the bike-and-skate rental place, housed in an old caboose.

Independent Politics (3 pts)

The alternative character of the town has even spread to the government, which funds things like the Village Meditation Program and sponsors neighborhood forums to hash out a philosophy for the future of the town.

Representatives on the village council are non-partisan and the village manager has an "open door" policy which welcomes criticism from residents.

The independent political posture of Yellow Springs has spread beyond its base of counterculture idealism. Even a corporation like

Yellow Springs Instrument, Inc. looks for different solutions to the same old problems. When its orders dropped in late 1990, YSI found itself with too little work for its employees.

Rather than the standard Wall Street solution, downsizing and layoffs, YSI cut the work week to 36 hours and filled the resulting downtime with classes in adult education. The company saw the education expense as a means to improve performance of its self-directed production teams.

Freedom of the Bedroom (2 pts)

Yellow Springs is one of the smallest municipalities to pass comprehensive legislation barring discrimination based on sexual orientation. Antioch College was caricatured in the national news a few years ago, with its politically correct sexual conduct code. But back on the street, I overheard the following conversation between passersby.

Man: Hey, baby, you smell great!

Woman (smiling): So do you.

One of the many avenues of research for this book involved tracking down utopian communities. Sadly, the self-conscious experiments in utopia I was able to uncover are now all as dead as Latin, or maybe Esperanto. However, if any one place in my contemporary explorations is moving nearer to utopia, in an unassuming way, it is Yellow Springs, which might be nicknamed "Mellow Springs."

But how will it resolve its dilemma? If it remains small, will it lose its diversity? Or if it expands, will it lose its distinct character? Or, will it discover a third way?

TOTAL POINTS: 25

ALSO-ELIGIBLE PLACES

Some places should readily qualify for this book but their intrinsic characteristics are such that they defy our rating system. They may be "overqualified" in one of the categories but lack the dimensions in others. They may be too ambiguous or undefined geographically. Or they may be in a state of rapid transition.

In racing, horses that may or may not get into a race are called also-eligibles. This is the term that shall be used in reference to the unscored places that follow.

CAFÉ THEME PARK: SEATTLE, WASHINGTON

Sure, Seattle is a beautiful place, great views, lots of exciting ups and downs, cultured, chic. This isn't a book about "in" places, but Seattle has at least one avant-garde trait. A coffee revolution has been brewing in Seattle. And the revolution is spreading.

When the number of cafés began to escalate in New York, it was mentioned that the city was becoming "Seattle-ized." Most travel guides, in one way or another, highlight that gourmet coffee has become a trademark of Seattle.

A tourist flying cross country to visit Seattle was heard to say that he was going there to have a cup of "café latté," Seattle's own version of capuccino.

But Seattle's espresso madness has reached a new extreme with the publication of a guidebook written solely about the city's coffee: *Seattle Emergency Espresso*, by Heather Doran Barbieri.

Seattle, with its theme cafés, has outdone Disney. Within the city's most alternative neighborhood alone, Capitol Hill (about a 15-minute bus ride east of downtown), there is a classical music café (Stravinsky European Café & Espresso Bar), a provocative art work café (Puss-Puss Café), a livingroom café with a fake fireplace (Rosebud Espresso), a gas station relic café (Museum Café & Ethyl Deli), a café to slow down your life (Adagio Espresso)...get it?, a romantic, poetic café (B&O Espresso), an environment-conscious café (Beans), a gay-and-straight café (Cause Celebre), a kosher café (Matzoh Mamma), an organic café (Java Joe's Espresso Cart), a wall-mural café (Café Paradiso), and even an all-American café (Capitol Hill Diner).

And those are just a few.

In the same way that some folks might feel that Disney's New Orleans is better than the real New Orleans, one could argue that Seattle's café scene is better than its European model.

Having lived in Paris, I was able to observe that some of the more interesting old-continent cafés would be considered "dives" or "joints" by our standards. Several of the cafés in my neighborhood didn't even have names. Sure, there were mosaic tiles here and there, or fine woodwork, or stained glass, but you hardly noticed these things because the smoke was thick and blue, or the decor was too busy to pick out distinguishing details, or the place was simply too dirty, including bathrooms with toilets that consisted of two metallic plates shaped like feet and in between, a hole in the floor.

Alright Seattle, try installing a bathroom like that in one of your cafés!

Yes, there are more distinguished looking cafés in Paris, but the most spirited neighborhood hangouts were the ones I described. And when people went in to ask for a café express, or a café au lait, there was nothing religious about the whole thing. It was simply a cup of coffee. Good coffee, to be sure, but nothing more. I guess in the States we've been poured tinted water for so many years that when good coffee finally comes along, it's a real event.

But this is all too unfair. Seattle has a right and a duty to create radiant cafés, so that the inhabitants can step in out of the nine grey months of rain and mist. I apologize. Theme park is unfair. Seattle is to café what Bordeaux is to wine. And if the French can be religious about their wineries, then folks in Seattle have a right to worship their frothy café latté and to sip it with delight.

As a coffee lover, I like what has happened in Seattle, and am glad the custom is beginning to spread across the country.

But Danny, a Seattle resident, is becoming fearful of café fundamentalists.

"In Seattle," he told me, "when they find out I don't drink coffee, I get the feeling they want to run me out of town."

CITY OF COMMERCE, CALIFORNIA

City of Commerce offers an alternative to urban, suburban or country life, the chance to be one of the few lucky homeowners or renters to live in an area dominated by heavy and light industry. If one allows pure imagery to replace the meaning of things, the landscape of smoke stacks, wire fences and the bizarre geometry of immense grey factories becomes a dynamic, abstract mural. With only 6.6 percent of the space in City of Commerce set aside for residence, as opposed to 63.8% for industry, weirdos who decide to make a home here in essence are living in an industrial park.

In exchange for their willingness to reside in the absurd penumbra of the industrial revolution, inhabitants are granted the privilege of paying no city property tax, nor utilities tax. They are treated to a free city-wide bus system and become eligible for all types of low-interest loans.

For added ambience, there is an imposing medieval structure that serves as a town center. Once occupied by the Uniroyal Tire and Rubber factory, its 35 acres were subject to a massive environmental clean-up. Now called The Citadel, it houses 40 retail outlets, several restaurants, four office buildings and a hotel. There is no funkier combination than a pre-industrial castle complex in a post-industrial setting.

City of Commerce is an enclave in East Los Angeles, with an influential Mexican-American presence, and an active sister-city affiliation with Aguascalientes, Mexico.

Long before casinos had spread beyond Las Vegas and Atlantic City, this city had broken the taboo against gambling, opening the Commerce Casino, with five varieties of poker (lowball, draw, Texas hold 'em, seven-card stud and Omaha) as well as four Asian games (pan, Asian poker, super pan 9 and pai gow).

But the best bets of City of Commerce are the economic amenities it offers those valiant pioneers who stake their claim in a forest of smokestacks.

DOWN AND OUT IN CAMBRIDGE, MASSACHUSETTS

With Harvard University, M.I.T. and Radcliffe College all in Cambridge, Massachusetts, this city of 100,000 inhabitants, just across the Charles River from Boston, is the breeding ground of the aristocracy. Look at the young faces in any of the city's hip restaurants and cafés and you will be seeing future cabinet members, CEOs and high-powered attorneys.

Precisely which of these faces will be appearing on Meet the Press or in the *Wall Street Journal* is not yet apparent, but it is inevitable that some of them will make it.

On the streets outside what Cambridge publicists call a "culinary bonanza" with Italian, Greek, Caribbean, Chinese, Korean, Creole, Portugese, stir fried, spicy and "equatorial," is a ragtag army of hungry people, numbering around 700.

There is a guidebook called *Historic Walks in Cambridge*, which requires 390 pages; so dense is this city with historic structures that the so-called "walk" becomes a historic standstill. This is a high-rent city, which is one of the various reasons why there are so many homeless. Cambridge has rent control, "but that's an ongoing joke," says homeless advocate Jim Stewart. "The mayor lives in a rent-control apartment!"

Stewart is soft-spoken but the words of this commited activist are fighting mad, mainly because the plight of the homeless "doesn't seem to incense the population here. Ironic," he adds, "since people wear T-shirts declaring that the most opinionated people have the 02138 zip code."

Stewart speaks of a "double standard" based on whether you are amongst the elite or down and out. "If an indigent person makes a mistake, people want him to pay for it. But when the savings-and-loan scandals happened, no one holds those people morally responsible for what they did."

There is pain in Stewart's voice as he tells of the death of an indigent person following a police beating. "The inquest found that yes, the kick caused his head to hit the rail, but found no criminal intent.

"Cambridge is a place where indigent people are beaten by the police. Homeless people's lives count about as much as infected yeast."

He finds it ironic that bookstore owners who sell sociological treatises about the homeless don't want panhandlers outside their store, as if theoretical understanding is divorced from reality.

With all this, you'd think that we would write that Cambridge is a "city of contrasts." But that old cliché is simply an excuse to avoid confronting reality. The fact that there exists an elite (no one can deny that Harvard is the elite of the universities) means that there has to be a down-and-out. It just so happens that these two sectors converge in Cambridge.

Perhaps we'd edge a bit nearer the truth by suggesting that Cambridge is a city of contradictions. One of those contradictions is that homeless advocate Jim Stewart himself is a graduate of the elite University of Harvard's Divinity School. Or that the Phillips Brooks House at Harvard runs a winter shelter staffed by student volunteers, which provides the homeless with access to things like sports facilities and computers...as well as a 7-week temporary summer shelter. What an irony that the homeless provide Harvard with a way out of the ivory tower, with a slice of reality missing from other more sheltered schools.

Stewart readily admits that after allowing about a week to get a grip on reality, the students do a good job.

Various shelters, including the First Church shelter where Stewart works, are run by religious institutions.

"The religious community," Stewart adds, "deserves a lot of credit for having shamed the city into taking some resonsibility."

It was like telling them, "You can't claim to be this enlightened, hip community if you continually dump these problems on the private sector."

As a result, the city started the Cambridge Multi-Service Center, which helps homeless people stabilize their lives.

One reason that Cambridge is indeed a hip place is the presence of another down and out segment of the population, this one living on the margins intentionally. This sector produces a countercultural street scene of musicians, puppeteers and the likes.

The marginals-by-choice and the homeless interact at places like the Naked City Coffee House, where homeless people are served for free and invited to read their poetry.

A group called Bread and Jam provides free dinners and a self-help center for the homeless, including resumé assistance and a "blind answering service" so that potential employers will not know that they are calling a shelter.

Jim Stewart has shared all this information, so his message remains contradictory. Cambridge is and isn't insensitive to the homeless. Homelessness itself is not the monolithic thing it is made out to be. In fact, there are even college grads amongst the homeless. One of them had been a taxi driver in New York who was shot point-blank in the head and left to die. He survived but he now has trouble convincing himself that the world is worth the effort. As he puts it, he cares too much in a world that cares too little.

There is visible evidence that the efforts at stabilizing the indigent in Cambridge are paying off. Homeless and former homeless people even produce a newspaper, called *Spare Change*.

In tourist books, you just don't read about the Naked City Coffee House or the Phillips Brooks House or the Christ Church shelter or Jim Stewart or the First Church shelter or Bread and Jam or *Spare Change*. Cambridge is much more than simply a city of elite universities, exciting restaurants and historic buildings; it is much more complex and challenging than that.

ECOVILLAGE, ITHACA, NEW YORK

EcoVillage is the most ambitious environment-conscious community to be conceived in the United States. Derived from cohousing, a form of cooperative living developed in Denmark, EcoVillage is designed to do minimum harm to the planet while offering an alternative to the alienating structure of modern suburbs.

Thirty pioneer families initiated the revolutionary living arrangement in 1995, with a population ultimately expected to reach 500.

A comparison with a typical suburb will help to illustrate the magnitude of the EcoVillage experiment. While suburbs are lucky to set aside 20 percent of the land for open space, EcoVillage raises that figure to 80 percent, including arable land, ponds and forests.

Meanwhile, the autmobile will no longer determine the streetscape; no more drab garages facing the street, no more the desolation of paved driveways. Instead, homes will be clustered, with parking off to the side.

Shared heating systems will be made adaptable to potential innovations that are projected to use renewable energy sources.

And rather than having people withdraw into the solitude and inefficiency of disjointed single-family houses, there will be a minimum of personal space, enough to protect one's privacy, with lots of common space instead, including washing-machine rooms, community kitchens and dining halls.

A number of the families moving into EcoVillage are downscaling the material part of their lives in order to enhance the human factor. They are thrilled to abandon their dependency on individual lawn mowers, snow blowers, leaf slurpers, and sundry devices. EcoVillage pioneers consider it redundant many times over for each family to have its own machinery.

While private space will be limited to the essential, areas where residents can escape, such as contemplation ponds with benches, will allow for the solitude needed to balance with the feel of community.

On the other hand, casual hangouts, what is lacking in most suburbs, will be prominent in EcoVillage, including reading rooms and chess rooms. Although most cooking can be done in a common kitchen, each home will be equiped with a small, private kitchen as well, with refrigerators half the normal size.

The project's founder, Joan Bokaer, explains that the ideas for conserving resources while enhancing the sense of community may still evolve. The goals are ambitious, with some temporary concessions needed in order to maintain reasonable prices. That means putting off a state-of-the-art waste treatment center for the time being and using Ithaca's sewers.

Thanks to the resource-conserving layout of EcoVillage, housing will be surprisingly affordable, with prices expected to begin at $83,000 for a two-bedroom unit. The projected price for a four-bedroom version is $121,000. Not bad!

Aware of the commune failures of past generations, the visionary planners of EcoVillage are not likely to be the victims of history repeating itself. There is a keen understanding of the need for balance between private and public space.

Meanwhile, back in the mainstream, the perceived need for unlimited privacy has left many folks so wrapped up in their own four walls that they now yearn to become part of a community once again.

GAITHERSBURG, MARYLAND

Drive off the 270 Freeway, 25 miles northwest of Washington, D.C., follow the signs for the Lakeforest Shopping Mall, pass a few cement-fortress department stores with no windows, standing within bleak parking lots. Cross the main strip, Route 355, gas stations and chain restaurants. We're in Alienationville, USA.

This is one face of Gaithersburg, Maryland, three Roy Rogers restaurants, KFC, a parking lot, McDonalds, a parking lot, Toys R Us and Montgomery Ward, another parking lot, Midas Muffler, another parking lot, Pizza Hut, another parking lot. The invasion that didn't happen in War of the Worlds is right here, in and around Route 355. The Martians look down on this and they say, who needs this? Foreigners take a bus tour across the country and they wonder how every place looks so much like this.

The first sign of any deviation from the norm occurs, oddly, outside the immense shopping mall parking lot. Canadian snow geese stroll in a long single file across the road and traffic is backed up. There is no grass roots community movement to limit the numbers of the snow geese, not even complaints about the shit they deposit on walking paths.

The Lakeforest Mall and its vast parking lot is a giant tumor that should have suffocated the city of Gaithersburg once and for all.

Less than a mile past the mall is downtown Gaithersburg. The town is entrenched in a silent war. How to maintain its own vitality in the shadow of the Mall. City officials added the letter "e" to its Old(e) Town(e), but fortunately it still looks more like an old town.

The Diamond Pharmacy features a greasy spoon lunch counter in a general store atmosphere, with 60's prices and 40's pre-espresso regulars. Food counter regulars are an integrated group, the first sign that we are not back in the forties. Mercifully, its parking lot is hidden in back, and it communicates directly with the street.

There are two old-fashioned barbershops, a food store, a Latin American grocery where they threw in my hot pepper for free when I bought tortillas and beans, various Asian restaurants, Faye's family restaurant, a Tai Chi and Yoga school, a Ben Franklin's department store, a city hall in an old Victorian home, a halfway house in another Victorian, and a vintage railroad depot, still in commuter use, with an outdoor museum consisting of an old black steam engine, a caboose, a mail car and a passenger car.

On most days, downtown is pretty quiet, but the local government sponsors street and ethnic fairs, a biweekly flea market, an eclectic line-up of summer concerts and an annual free Jazz Festival, of high quality but intimate spirit, where I was able to enchange a few words with Billy Taylor and get his autograph.

More recently, the Olde Towne Tavern and Brewing Company moved into a red-brick historic building, right across from Diamond Drugs. The yuppies have now found a lively microbrewery, with rock 'n' roll or jazz Saturday nights. Suddenly, downtown is drawing people in.

The downtown day shift centers around Diamond Pharmacy. Like clockwork, as the first shift (the lunch counter) winds down, the Tavern opens up to its new crowd, which spills out onto the street. I can envision the debut of a another club to take in the spillover Tavern crowd, and before you know it, Gburg becomes a night magnet for young adults and other seekers of good times.

A third Gaithersburg alternative is found at the end of town, just past a hardware store occupying an old granary building. This third face of Gaithersburg is hidden in thick woods and separated from Route 355 by the railroad.

It is called Washington Grove. At its edge, there is a post office, a feed store, the hardware store and a convenience store. Otherwise, this community, once a religious retreat, consists of a quirky array of porched houses from pre-development days, none of them younger than three quarters of a century. The streets are all narrow, some dark asphalt but many simply grass and gravel and primarily for pedestrians. Jogging there at midday, you can avoid the sun beneath green cathedral canopies. This is Gaithersburg's milder way of accomplishing what Wall Street and the Amazon Rainforest are famous for.

Washington Grove still maintains a "prohibition" ordinance, mainly to keep out liquor stores, although one resident told us, "That doesn't mean we don't know how to party."

A fourth alternative, on the other side of the mall, is Montgomery Village, a planned community dubbed "Tree City" for its wetlands preservation. Here the snow geese thrive. If you get too close to the lakes, turtles bathing on the rocks will skitter into the water. Most houses are bordered by woods, and you can stroll from one part of the Village to another over tree covered paths, all the while only yards from a main road. Occasionally, unschooled baby deer wander into a cluster of homes. A beaver builds a dam by night and hides by day.

The county has wanted to extend a leg of the freeway through the wetlands and upgrade an old one-lane, right-of-way bridge, but so far, the locals have fought off the incursions.

A small shopping center, also in competition with the mall, has a few budding hangouts in spite of its unfortunate parking lot. An outdoor arcade saves the center from being totally overwhelmed by the lot. Hangouts include a tattoo-and-country-western-crowd café, a yogurt shop that draws an outdoor crowd under the arcade, and a mini-plaza by the $1.99 movie theater.

The fifth dimension of Gaithersburg is Kentlands, a planned community intended as an alternative to the burbs. Unlike one-builder developments, this one employs ten different construction companies. It has been planned by the same architects responsible for Seaside, Florida, Elizabeth Plater-Zyberk and Andres Duany.

Some streets in Kentlands look like Georgetown: rows of townhouses with colorful dormers and various grainy brick textures; other streets conjure up the best of turn-of-the-century America. Kentlands' intimacy is due to the fact that garages have been banished to back alleys, houses are close to each other and to the street, and there are no cul-de-sacs (T-junctions protect the eye from void horizons).

The bad news is that Kentlands is "tres cher." If you want low rent, you have to search for pockets within Montgomery Village or in the downtown area, the two parts of Gaithersburg where a multi-cultural mix is an answer to the white bread suburban tracts farther north along Route 270.

It is rare to find a city of only 30,000 with five totally different faces: the mall and commercial strip, the downtown, Washington Grove, Montgomery Village, Kentlands. Some parts of Gburg are pedestrian friendly, with a public bus system connecting to the nearby D.C. Metro. There are a few notable hangouts here and there, and an occasional upended facility. The city government works hard to encourage a cross-cultural understanding and stepped in forcefully when a couple of hate crimes against Latins threatened the positive tenor of the town. Some of the most integrated and well-functioning schools in the whole state are found within the Gaithersburg umbrella.

Gaithersburg qualifies for this book because it contains five distinct personalities in one, four of which offer alternatives to the mainstream.

HARD-CORE LAS VEGAS, NEVADA

A Las Vegas trip inward goes from the tacky to the kinky to the funky. Most folks never get down to the third, innermost layer. Ostentatious theme park hotels, all-you-can-stuff-in buffets and slot machines in endless rows that look like cemeteries for dead brains: that's the tacky level.

With legal whorehouses beyond the county line, Las Vegas has to sell the image of sex rather than sex itself. But for overpriced "bell girls," you mainly get a peek or a leer, in exchange for consuming things other than sex, such as games of no chance or expensive bottles of champagne.

But there is an inner core of Las Vegas which offers state-of-the art aesthetics, that is, if you're a smart "gambler." The residents of this inner Las Vegas are guys, and a few women as well, who actually make ends meet by betting. They constitute an alternative subculture that floats in and out of the casinos, virtually invisible to most tourists.

These Las Vegas diehards have no use for shows, never touch the lever of a one-armed bandit, pass by keno games and roulette tables as if they were radio static, rarely vote in elections, and are either divorced or married to kindred souls.

They choose one of only three games that can be beaten: horse betting, sports betting and poker. (Blackjack was once a beatable game, before the casinos added decks to make card counting virtually impossible.)

There is not much crossover between the three genres, although there is a cross-genre mutual respect. The one hangout where this intelligentsia of Las Vegas finds a common ground is the Gamblers' Book Club (630 South 11th Street); the counterculture of serious gamblers, most of whom call themselves investors, finds a home away from home at GBC.

In particular, the race-and-sports betting crowd constitutes a loose community, since they are up against nationwide betting publics; this is not so for poker players, whose main rival is each other, except when they can find a table with easy prey. The community of sports and race "investors" is the primary foundation of the hard-core Las Vegas subculture.

Within the casinos, the race-and-sports books are authentic hangouts. Cocktail waitresses, ornately or scantily clad, depending on the casino, stride by comfortable rows of desks offering complimentary drinks, coffee, juice, sodas or harder stuff. Each "book" has its regulars, although a number of these serious players make it a habit of hanging out in two or even three of their preferred venues.

For "normal" players, a change of pace is going to the movies or white water rafting, but for the hard-core regulars, only a change of casino offers variety.

When Caesar's Palace and The Hilton began a trend of electronic race-and-sports betting emporiums, a number of these serious players abandoned the more traditional places such as the Barbary Coast, where the results are still written in by hand on sliding wall boards. But some of these cozier traditional race-and-sports books seem to be making a comeback.

Meanwhile, one of the original trendsetters in race and sports betting, the Stardust, still has its faithful legion, in part because you don't have to walk through a slot-machine obstacle course to get to the screens and betting area.

Most members of this subculture have been successful people in the "straight" world but have become disenchanted with corporate and government politics (or have simply desired a greater challenge in their lives), and have found refuge in the abstraction of gambling. They recognize that they have chosen a tough game, one that requires more work than a steady job. But they also recognize that the odds are the same for any and everybody who decides to try these games, and in this sense, they have found an alternative to the stacked-deck situations that infest the outside world.

Although basically apolitical, these people usually harbor a deep-seated scorn for traditional liberalism and conservatism, and if there were any one label that would apply the most, it would be libertarian.

Regional loyalty is also beneath them. They know that the Miami Dolphins or the Chicago Bears care whether we as individuals are rooting for them as much as the number three horse in the ninth race cares that we have bet on him.

Do these hard-core gamblers make a living at their craft? From my observations, I'd conclude that for some of them, gambling is their entire income, for a larger segment, production of racing or sports stats or books gives them a safety-net income, while still others make only a moderate income and barely subsist.

Even the losers in this subculture are part of the non-degenerate gambling intelligentsia; for the most part, once they discover that they cannot make it, they are smart enough to drop out from the serious game, go back to their other life and only gamble recreationally.

Many sports bettors shop around for the best line, or waiting through the week to see if they can get an extra point or half point in "the spread" on the games they prefer to bet.

For one who is not familiar with this subculture, it is possible to tell the difference between the pros and the degenerates by several measures. First, the degenerates are trying to get in bets on every race at every track, while the pros are extremely selective in their investments.

Then, the pros rarely jump up and shout as the horses come down the stretch or at the crucial moment when a field goal might win or lose the game according to the point spread. The pros know that this is a long-term business and the result of one game or race means little in the ultimate scheme of things. Clever analysis and not luck is the ultimate determining factor in success or failure.

Another way to pick out a pro, although this is more haphazard, is to look for a laptop computer. All pros keep meticulous records of their investments and many of them subscribe to online information services (but never tout services). On the other hand, some laptoppers expect too much from their machines and use them as a crutch, while a significant slice of the community of smart bettors remains in the pen-and-paper culture.

The preferred bet of most horseplayer pros in Las Vegas is the house quinella, whose payouts skim off less from the top than track quinellas or exactas. In these bets, the player must pick the top two horses in either order. Similarly, the smart bettors flock to sports books offering an extra edge in the odds.

Sports book owners used to believe that all horseplayers were degenerate. Only when the Sport of Kings Race Book lost a ton of money to smart horseplayers after having offered them better odds, did the race book managements realize that there was a significant subculture of discerning players out there. As a result, there is a trend afoot among the race book managers to scale back on promotions. The house quinella is now an endangered species. This bet has been "booked" by the casino and not tied into the larger pari-mutuel pools of the tracks.

In fact, most race books are now "going pari-mutuel," which means that it makes no difference whether the bettors win or lose since the race books receive a fixed-percentage cut based strictly on how much action they take in. Now the casino no longer puts a limit on payoffs of larger bets, nor does it ever refuse to take a bet.

For sports bettors it is probably tougher to find an extra edge. They must look for that rare time when a "line" is not objective, when they can get more "points" on a game than they deserve to get. Such a scenario would not be due to an error of Roxy Roxborough, whose lines are the most accurate in the world. But Roxy's lines reflect how the public is projected to bet. An "advantageous" line for the smart bettor is one where the public psychology, relative to the game, is likely tilted in the wrong direction. Roxy may know that Notre Dame should be a two point underdog to Boston College, but he also knows that the public will be betting on the Notre Dame mistique, so he must make Notre

Dame the favorite. A perfect line results in the sports book taking in an equal amount of wager money on each team.

For most folks, Las Vegas is a place to unload money and then rationalize that they had a good time. For the hard-core Las Vegas subculture, it offers the most comfortable and informative setting for their occupation. I asked one of these gamblers why he chose to live in a desert where it gets up to 118 degrees in the summer.

He could care less about the weather, since the race-and-sports books are climate controlled.

"Back in my home town," he responded, "I felt like a space cadet. No one could conceive that I was dead serious about what I was doing. They assumed that I was a degenerate.

"Here in Las Vegas, there are other serious players like me. Sure, we're rivals in a certain sense, but at least I feel less estranged in what I'm doing."

Surprisingly, most of these pros are remarkably well-rounded people, but the ones who reside in Las Vegas have decided to focus exclusively on their quest, a virtual obligation given the demanding nature of their art.

The proven winners in this subculture must still contend with the limited focus of their endeavor, whose psychological ups and downs become more tempestuous since they unfold in such a confined psychic space.

An early morning desert jog or dinner in one of Las Vegas' more interesting Vietnamese or Basque restaurants (as far from The Strip as possible) offer some degree of alleviation.

SOUTH BRONX

South Bronx was the prototypical example of the decayed inner city. After the past 20 years of a disintegrating industrial core and a fleeing middle class tax base, the neighborhood has been given up for dead, as exemplified by its gruesome portrayal in Tom Wolfe's novel, *The Bonfire of the Vanities*, as well as in various "urban jungle" movies.

At a time when other areas of the country are revitalizing their inner city baseball parks, George Steinbrenner is threatening to move out of Yankee Stadium, the home of the Bronx Bombers, complaining that suburbanites who come to see the games are scared of the neighborhood.

The South Bronx was so far down that its only way was up. I had heard rumors of revival simmering in various parts of this largely minority neighborhood (44 percent Latino, 37 percent African American), so I got off my Amtrak train at 125th Street in Harlem and rode the subway up to South Bronx.

I visited Hostos Community College and its recently inaugurated arts complex, the focal point in borough president Fernando Ferrer's Bronx Center Project, which covers a 300-block area from 147th to

169th streets.

Hostos is the first visible evidence of a rebirth in South Bronx. It follows the rehabilitation or demolition of all the infamous vacant buildings that had been threats to public safety.

Unlike many urban culture centers which develop a social-fortress disposition that separates them from the community at large, the Hostos arts center intends to act as a cultural anchor. It has already developed a strong interaction with the community and its local artists, blending culture, education and community activism as a means to lift up the neighborhood.

Bernd Zimmermann, a visionary planner active in the revitalization explained to me that the Bronx's plan is to "get rid of the psychological, social and physical barriers" that have plagued urban renewal projects of the past.

Indirectly, the Hostos vision emerged from a health revolt at decaying Lincoln Hospital, where part of the facility was taken over by local activists. The medical staff used Maoist philosophy as the foundation for drug detox therapy. These activists were among the conceivers of the original plan for Hostos.

The arts center is a comfortable place to be. Its animated pedestrian pathways pass over the Grand Concourse and then beneath and between several floors of balconies, as if it were the center of a Spanish village.

With neighborhood theater projects involving families from the community, and with the expectation of attracting graphic- and performance-arts related businesses, the Hostos arts center is intended to stimulate the local economy.

As it is, the community had never really died. *The Village Voice* refers to the Grand Concourse as "a once magnificent boulevard —based on the design of the Champs Elysees and dotted with Art Deco glory that would humble the now trendy streets of South Miami Beach." Within the part of town labeled South Bronx, there are seven areas designated as historic districts. At least two of these districts have a healthy ethnic mix.

The Hostos arts center is helped by the fact that the theater infrastructure already exists. One example is "Pregones," an eclectic Puerto Rican theater and ballet group that has an established reputation in downtown Manhattan and in various cities in the Northeast.

More controversial are the approximately 50 "casitas" (little houses) which function as cultural centers but are viewed by the city as squatters' camps, since they operate in ramshackle structures pieced together in the urban wilderness of empty lots.

These casitas act as a magnet for Puerto Rican folk artists, musicians and dancers, and as a regular stop for Latino musicians from outside of New York. The "foundation" of the casitas is a "music akin to American blues and rooted in the songs of cane cutters—which blossomed around the turn of the century when

Caribbean blacks migrated from the fields to the cities."

Ironically, the casitas in the empty lots are a "comfortable" escape from the drab, high-rise projects; yet, the city doesn't see it that way, and only time will tell whether community groups lobbying in favor of the casitas will win their struggle. At the moment, the Department of City Planning, at the urging of Borough representatives, has made room for a new casita to replace an old one, Rincón Criollo, that had to come down. They are attempting in earnest to preserve the atmosphere of the original casita.

South Bronx has always been a fascinating place. Its reputation has dissuaded many people from an enriching visit.

This reputation may change if the Hostos arts center is successful with even a portion of its plans. A further irony is that Hostos College is located only a few blocks south of the infamous Bronx courthouse building lampooned by Tom Wolfe.

With a philosophy similar to the Hostos venture, the Master Plan for Yankee Stadium sees the stadium as an anchor that weaves into the fabric of the community, rather than an isolated fortress.

The Bronx is the only New York borough with a Preservation Task Force. Everyone knew about the South Bronx when it was the butt of all jokes. But now that it is well on its way to an amazing comeback, few people notice.

We are on shaky ground when trying to score a place that finds itself in a dynamic process of transformation, so South Bronx will remain unrated.

SUSQUEHANNA RIVER ISLANDS, HARRISBURG, PENNSYLVANIA

Completed in 1901, the Rockville Bridge is still the world's longest stone arch bridge, crossing the Susquehanna River just north of Harrisburg, Pennsylvania. From the bridge, during warm weather, one can observe people wading in the middle of this wide river. From the shore, the waders look like so many distant stars of bright colors. The shallowness that allows this to happen is mainly a result of the age of the river: 200 million years.

Aside from fishing for large-mouth striped bass and the small mouth bass typical of this region, what are the river denizens up to? Most of the Susquehanna's numerous islands, where the waders seem to be going, are uninhabited. The Fish and Game Commission classifies those islands as wilderness.

In a recent court case, a convicted drug dealer testified that he had hid his merchandise on one of the islands in the Susquehanna. Some locals assert that evidence of witchcraft rituals has been found on some islands. A Fish and Game Commission agent told me that on weekends there are people out there partying. Rumors of orgies have surfaced.

The dilemma is: who has jurisdiction over the islands? The Fish and Game Commission agent explained to me that the question of jurisdiction remains to be decided, thanks to the fact that William Penn himself had failed to clarify which islands belong to whom.

At the moment, the Fish and Game Commission is attempting to sort out the mess, with lengthy and painstaking research. But in the meantime, the agent adds:

"Some families have gone so far as to claim their island or piece of one. We call them squatters."

In other words, on these islands, there is no government. Anarchy is not just a theory here. It is the objective reality.

The government is progressing slowly in searching for a way to bring the law of the land to the islands of the Susquehanna. When gays were using an island just off Harrisburg as a romantic retreat, the government stepped in and created an amusement park and baseball stadium on what is now called City Island.

Another inroad of "civilization" on the Susquehanna Islands is the infamous Three Mile Island, a few miles south of Harrisburg, scene of a nearly catastrophic "event" on March 28, 1979. One of the island's reactors still lies idle as a result of that accident.

It is ironic that the state government should take an interest in bringing the islands under some sort of law and order, since the magnificent Pennsylvania State Capitol, with its soaring dome patterned after St. Peter's Basilica in Rome, was born of a monumental graft scandal, when only four of the thirteen million dollars spent on the project actually went into construction.

But at that time, four million went a long way. The spectacular dome is but one highlight of the Capitol. There are marble staircases with wrought-iron railings, inspired by the Paris Opera House. Gilded and vaulted ceilings and red floor tiles inlaid with scenes of Pennsylvania life come from various other artistic periods.

The naked statues on either side of the entrance to the Capitol have innocuous formal descriptions, such as "the spiritual burdens carried by mankind," but if Jesse Helms gets wind that these erotic figures were paid for out of government funds, we would surely hear from him.

In other words, the islands (with a small "i") of the Susquehanna have a fitting accompaniment along the shore: beyond-the-law real estate deals and sensual imagery.

Another Susquehanna monument is Enola ("alone" spelled backwords), where the parallel-to-the-river railroad tracks of a 4.5 mile freight facility glisten in the setting sun. At Enola's historic peak, 3,000 cars were routed each day.

The Susquehanna River also begets all kinds of monuments to the American Pastime. Its source is Cooperstown, home of the Baseball Hall of Fame. After moving lazily south, it reaches Williamsport, home of the only truly "world" series, where little league teams from all over the planet come to participate. Farther south, off the shore from Harrisburg, there is minor league baseball on City Island.

Baseball, freight yards, nuclear power plants, monuments of corruption: the Susquehanna region is an exciting slice of the USA. But most seducing of all are the islands, a last frontier of unbridled freedom.

If the government ever gets its act together and civilizes all the islands, the last unpoliced region of Pennsylvania will be relegated to history. In the meantime, if you're thinking of wading out to your own little romantic island for two (or three), make sure you've cleared out the poison ivy before you start rolling around. And on the way, watch your step. There are some huge river clams that hang out on the bed of the Susquehanna.

WHEELING, WEST VIRGINIA

In many cities across this nation, the silent war between the chains and family businesses is over. The chains have won and the downtowns where ma and pa used to thrive are now dead.

In Wheeling, a northern city in a southern state, this war should have been over long ago. A regional mall, a commercial strip along Route 40 and freeways that allow the traveler to bypass the town should have ravaged Wheeling once and for all.

But if you take a walk through the center of town, as well as up and around the surrounding neighborhoods, you soon discover that this is a seductive place. This is time travel, back to the early 1950s, but for a few modern buildings that have hardly scarred the Victorian unity of the place. There are neighborhood bars with pool tournaments and zesty pizza, there are people in the streets and there's an enticing "centre market" on a plaza.

Before we get too idyllic, it is true that some businesses have vacated downtown. "Yeah, we've been malled alright," said the owner of The Paradox Book Store, a local author of drama and poetry, who helped sponsor well-attended poetry readings, even one where they read works of the most exquisitely kinky poet of our times, Charles Bukowski. A hundred people showed up for that reading, 250 to a Dylan Thomas night. You don't find those crowds at poetry readings in L.A. or Chicago.

But how did the downtown and surrounding neighborhoods survive the battle and maybe the war too? I have a theory involving the juxtaposition of several factors.

First, Wheeling's geography is compact. On one side is the Ohio River. On the other, steep hills. I drove up one of them and found that the city ended there. Modern cities don't end, they thin out over an extended area. So Wheeling's geography makes it an intimate place that simply can't spill out.

Unlike Burlington, Vermont, for example, Wheeling has no controlled-growth policy. But the geography seems to accomplish the feat by itself.

Second, anchored in downtown there's the Capitol Music Hall, whose ornate architecture recalls the old Paris Opera, but with a bright American marquee. The Capitol Music Hall hosts Jamboree USA, now in its 57th year, the second oldest live radio broadcast in the country. Live radio variety shows are an anachronism in the TV age, but WWVA, whose powerful signal is heard all the way up into Canada, has kept the tradition alive.

Finally, there are three different groups in town, Friends of Wheeling, Victorian Wheeling Society and Victorian Landmarks Association that have acted as a counterforce in the economic tug-of-war between the downtown neighborhoods and the suburbs.

Wheeling is an unusual place. It is the nation's smallest city to support a metropolitan class symphony orchestra. Its luxurious gambling facility, a dog track, offers horse race simulcasting from the best tracks in the country. You can't get that in Los Angeles, for example. Its bridge over the Ohio River is a monument to steel sculpture, and you can walk across. In fact, everything is within walking distance in this compact city.

Culturally, Wheeling doesn't venture on the fringe of things. But it remains a lively anachronism, a classic American city that won't give in. It was the site of Nixon's Checkers Speech, and it seems that the city has not lost much of its unprocessed and unpretentious beauty since that infamous moment in history.

FINAL WORD

Readers who know of funky places that should have been included in this book are invited to submit their ratings of cities, towns or communities for possible inclusion in the next edition.

FINAL TALLIES

PRIMARY RATINGS

40	Mission District, San Francisco, California
39	New Orleans, Louisiana
37	Arcata, California
37	Key West, Florida
37	Venice, California
34	West Berkeley, California
31	Upcountry-Paia, Maui, Hawaii
30	Imperial Beach, California
30	Notsosoho, New York
29	Adams-Morgan, Washington, D.C.
28	Portland, Oregon
28	Taos, New Mexico
27	El Paso/Juarez, Texas/Mexico
27	Santa Fe, New Mexico
26	Rogers Park, Chicago, Illinois
25	Hoboken, New Jersey
25	Nome, Alaska
25	Yellow Springs, Ohio
23	Austin, Texas
23	Burlington, Vermont
23	Takoma Park, Maryland
22	Downtown Los Angeles, California
22	New Paltz, New York
22	Royal Oak, Michigan
19	Clarksdale, Mississippi
18	Columbus, New Mexico
18	Jerome, Arizona
18	Ocracoke, North Carolina
17	Eureka Springs, Arkansas
16	Berea, Kentucky
15	Ward, Colorado
14	Cajun Country, Louisiana
14	Elko, Nevada
14	Lily Dale, New York
14	Park City, Utah
13	Applegate Valley, Oregon
13	Genesee County, New York
13	New York Mills, Minnesota
12	Harpers Ferry, West Virginia
12	Hopland, California
12	Lopez Island and North Puget Sound, Washington
12	Sandy Hook, New Jersey
12	Seaside, Florida

11   Love Canal, New York
11   Madawaska, Maine
10   Ely, Nevada

SECONDARY RATINGS: THE ELEVEN BEST
The point system represents a multi-perspective composite of each place's funky and alternative characteristics. In order to satisfy distinct preferences and persuasions, *FunkyTowns USA* offers its "eleven best" within various optional rating categories. Each group of eleven will be presented in alphabetical order.

Best Places in Smallest Packages
The primary rating system favors larger places or communities situated within great urban areas. If the size factor were neutralized, which places would come out on top?
Arcata, California
Clarksdale, Mississippi
Elko, Nevada
Eureka Springs, Arkansas
Jerome, Arizona
New Paltz, New York
New York Mills, Minnesota
Ocracoke, North Carolina
Royal Oak, Michigan
Ward, Colorado
Yellow Springs, Ohio

Most Dynamic Cultural Mix
Adams-Morgan, Washington, D.C.
El Paso, Texas
Hoboken, New Jersey
Key West, Florida
New Orleans, Louisiana
Rogers Park, Chicago
Santa Fe, New Mexico
Taos, New Mexico
Upcountry-Paia, Maui, Hawaii
West Berkeley, California
Venice, California

Best Refuge for Misfits and Non-conformists
Applegate Valley, Oregon
Arcata, California
Imperial Beach, California
Key West, Florida

Mission District, San Francisco, California
New Orleans, Louisiana
New Paltz, New York
Nome, Alaska
Royal Oak, Michigan
Venice, California
West Berkeley, California

Most Audacious Social Policies
Berea, Kentucky
Burlington, Vermont
EcoVillage, New York
Genesee County, New York
Hopland, California
Portland, Oregon
Seaside, Florida
South Bronx, New York
Takoma Park, Maryland
Ward, Colorado
West Berkeley, California

Most Exciting
Adams-Morgan, Washington, D.C.
Cajun Country, Louisiana
Downtown Los Angeles, California
El Paso, Texas
Hoboken, New Jersey
Key West, Florida
Mission District, San Francisco, California
New Orleans, Louisiana
Notsosoho, New York
Upcountry-Paia, Maui
Venice, California

Most Benign Climate
Where you can't fry an egg on the sidewalk in the summer nor get whipped by a blizzard in the winter...west is best.
Arcata, California
Café Theme Park: Seattle, Washington
Imperial Beach, California
Lopez Island, Washington
Mission District, San Francisco, California
Portland, Oregon
Santa Fe, New Mexico
Taos, New Mexico
Upcountry-Paia, Maui
West Berkeley, California
Venice, California

BIBLIOGRAPHY

Aeppel, Timothy, "Housing Cooperative is Grown Naturally," *Wall Street Journal*, July 28, 1994, p. B1.

"At the Crossroads. Clarksdale, Mississippi," *The Economist*, July 11, 1992, p. A27.

Ballance, Alton. *Okracokers*. Chapel Hill: University of North Carolina Press, 1989.

Boit, John H., "Hope, Not Revenge," *Echoes*, Summer, 1992.

Boyer, Richard and Savageau, David. *Places Rated Almanac*. New York: Prentice Hall, 1988 (Eighth Edition).

Brandes Gratz, Roberta. *The Living City*. New York: Simon & Schuster, 1989.

Breslin, Jimmy, "North of the Border," *Travel-Holiday*, February 1993, p. 88.

Brown, Michael H., "A Toxic Ghost Town," *The Atlantic*, July,1989, pp. 23-28.

Cantor, George. *Where The Old Roads Go*. New York: Harper & Row, 1990.

Caughey, Bruce and Winstanky, Dean. *The Colorado Guide*. Golden, Colorado: Fulcrum Publishing, 1994.

Charlier, Marj, "Residents Fight to Tone Down Gissied-up, Gentrified Santa Fe," *The Wall Street Journal*, June 20, 1994, p. B1.

Clarke, Thurston, "The Key to Romance," *Travel-Holiday*, November 1993, pp. 80-88.

Crampton, Norman, *The 100 Best Small Towns in America*. New York: Prentice Hall, 1993.

Curtiss, Aaron, "Grand Hopes for City Core," *Los Angeles Times*, January 9, 1994, p. B3.

DaRosa, Allison, "Lopez Locals Savor the Simple, Unhurried Island Lifestyle," *San Diego Union-Tribune*, Sunday. July 17, 1994, Travel Section, p. 1-2.

Draper, Robert, "Remains of the Desert," *American Way*, November 15, 1994, p. 96.

Frazier, Ian, "On Urban Shores," *The New Yorker*, January 10, 1994.

Graves, Bill, "Ely, Nevada," *Trailer Life*, August 1993, p. 24-30.

Hamilton, William B., "Return of the Native Blues," *Washington Post*, January 14, 1992, Sec. E. p. 1.

Hamlin, Susan, "A Culinary Woodstock Celebrates the Garden," *The New York Times*, July 6, 1994.

Hart, Steven, "Sandy Hook Journal," *New York Times*, November 15, 1992.

Heartland: A Free American Journal, Number 42, Summer, 1994.

Hillerman, Tony. *New Mexico, Rio Grande and other Essays*. Portland, Oregon: Graphic Arts Publishing, 1992.

Hinz, Greg, "Generation Blender: Old and Young will Live Together in a Unique Rogers Park Residence," *Chicago*, April 23, 1994, p. 22.

Hirschorn, Michael, "Lost in the Funhouse," *Esquire*, January 1993, p. 49.

Holmstrom, David, "Life Among the Homeless," *Christian Science Monitor*, January 31, 1994, p. 11.

Horan, Kevin, "Windy City Fish Story," *Life*, May, 1994, p. 90.

Horwitz, Tem. *Sweet Home Chicago*. Chicago: Chicago Review Press, 1993, pp. 25-26.

Jenkins, Mark and Rice, Bill, "Lights! Camera! Parking!" *Washington City Paper*, February 11, 1994, p. 10.

Kunstler, James Howrd. *The Geography of Nowhere*. New York: Simon & Schuster, 1993.

La Ganga, Maria L, "Seeking Gold in the Silver State," *Los Angeles Times*, June 10, 1994, p. A1.

Lamb, David. *A Sense of Place*. New York: Random House, 1993.

Langdon, Philip, "How Portland Does It: a City that Protects its Urban Core," *New Yorker*, November, 1992, pp. 134-138.

Langdon, Philip. *A Better Place to Live*. Amherst: University of Massachusetts Press, 1994.

Leerhsen, Charles, "The Naked and the Dread," *Newsweek*, Sept. 10, 1990, p. 60.

Linnell, Pat, "The Wickedest Town in the West," *Trailer Life*, January 1994, p. 82.

Los Angeles Times. Various articles, with direct quote from a letters to the editor, Donald F. McIntyre (January 9, 1994) and Suzan Kern (June 8, 1994).

McDarrah, Fred W and Patrick J. *The Greenwich Village Guide*. New York: A Capella Books, 1994.

McIntyre, Donald F., "Downtown L.A." *Los Angeles Times*, p. B6.

McPhail, Robert, "Council Meeting Hall, Imperial Beach," *The San Diego Reader*," September 9, 1988.

Miller, Bryan, "Down Home in Acadiana," *New York Times Magazine-The Sophisticated Traveler*, March 6, 1992, p. S58.

Miller, Holly, "S'no Wonder," *The Saturday Evening Post*, p. 76.

Miller, Peter, "Susquehanna: America's Small-Town River," *National Geographic*, March, 1985, pp. 352-383.

Morales, Ed, "Can the Hostos Arts Center Spark Urban Renewal?" *Village Voice*, October 25, 1994, p. 35.

Morgan, Susan, "Life in Venice, California," *Interview*, June, 1993, p. 58.

Nathan, Debbie, "El Paso Under the Blockade," *The Nation*, February 28, 1994, p. 268.

Nieves, Evelyn, "Learning to love Love Canal again," *The New York Times*, July 12, 1984.

North Carolina Traveler, Edited by Ginny Turner. Winston-Salem: John F. Blair, Publisher, 1989.

The North Country Fair: A Collective Memory. Book published by the residents of Arcata.

Oldenburg, Ray. *The Great Good Place*. New York: Marlowe & Company, 1989.

Pacelle, Mitchell, "An Oasis of Island Culture Under Siege in the Bronx," *Wall Street Journal*, February 24, 1994.

Parfit, Michael, "The Hard Ride of Route 93," *National Geographic*, December, 1992, p. 52.

Powell, Padgett, "Eccentric, Authentic New Orleans," *New York Times Magazine-The Sophisticated Traveler*, October 18, 1992, p. S71.

Proctor, Mary and Matuszeski, Bill. *Gritty Cities*. Philadelphia: Temple University Press, 1978.

Rosenberg, Lee and Saralee. *50 Fabulous Places to Raise Your Family*. New York: Career Press, 1993.

Rough Guide USA. Various editions.

San Francisco and the Bay Area On the Loose (The Berkeley Guides). New York: Fodor's Travel, 1994.

Sancton, Thomas, "Why the Good Times Still Roll," *Time*, November 4, 1991, p. 36.

"Santa Fe's Flea Market," *Sunset*, March, 1992, p. 44.

Sinclair, Mick. *Florida Rough Guide*. 1993.

Smith, Griffin, "The Cajuns: Still Loving Life," *National Geographic*, October, 1990, pp. 40-65.

Strecker, Zoe. *Kentucky Off the Beaten Path*. Connecticut: Globe Pequot Press, 1992, pp. 23-24.

Sullivan, Robert, "Portland Postcard: Thorny," *The New Republic*, July 4, 1994, p. 9.

The Talk of the Town, "States of Undress," *The New Yorker*, June 14, 1993.

Tucker, Amy and Tanzer, Stephen, "All the Best and None of the Worst of Santa Fe, *Forbes*, Sept 27, 1993, p. S116.

Turan, Kenneth, "Sundance Fest Retains its Counterculture Essence," *Los Angeles Times*, January 26, 1994, Sec: F, p. 1.

Underwood, Anne, "The Return to Love Canal: would you move there?" *Newsweek*, July 30, 1990, p. 25.

Van Gelder, Sarah, "Genesee Peacemakers," *In Context*, a quarterly of humane sustainable culture, Spring 1994, pp. 35-38.

Villani, John. *The 100 Best Small Art Towns in America*. Santa Fe, New Mexico: John Muir Publications, 1994.

Walter, Jonathan, "National Sprawl Busters Coalition Emerges," *Historic Preservation News*, January, 1995, pp. 10-12.

Warren, Jennifer, "Cycling Reaches Critical Mass," *Los Angeles Times*, June 30, 1994, p. A3.

White, Mel, "Songs of the Ozarks," *National Geographic Traveler*, July-August, 1994, p. 84.

"Wildcat Academy, Class of 1994," *N.Y. Times*, July 11, 1994, B2.

Wilkie, Curtis, "Blues Get Devotion in Delta," *Boston Globe*, February 15, 1994, p. 3.

Wright, James G, "Residents Fear Utah Ski Town is going Downhill," *L.A. Times*, December 6, 1993, Sec: A, p. 5.

Yellow Springs News, September 15, 1994.

York, Byron, "Where the Blues were Born," *Washington Post*, July 4, 1993, Sec. E, p. 1.

PRIMARY INFORMATION INDEX

PHONE DIRECTORY

Sources for free information on tourism, relocation and retirement (Abbreviations: Chamber of Commerce, C/C; Convention Center and Visitors Bureau, CCVB).

Adams-Morgan, DC, Visitor Information Center	202/789-7038
Applegate Valley, OR, Grants Pass C/C	503/476-7717
Arcata, CA, C/C	707/822-3619
Austin, TX, CCVB	512/474-5171
Berea, KY, Tourism Commission	606/986-2540
Burlington, VT, Lake Champlain C/C	802/863-3489
Cajun Country, LA, Eunice C/C	800/222-2342
Breaux Bridge C/C	318/332-5406
Cambridge, MA, Cambridge Discovery	617/497-1630
City of Commerce, CA, C/C	213/728-7222
Clarksdale, MS, Coahoma Tourism Commission	800/626-3764
Columbus, NM, C/C	505/531-2708
Eco-Village, NY, Ithaca CCVB	800/284-8422
El Paso, TX, CCVB	915/534-0696
Elko NV, C/C	702/738-7135
Ely, NV, White Pine C/C	702/289-8877
Eureka Springs, AR, C/C	501/253-8737
Gaithersburg, MD, C/C	301/840-1400
Genesee County, NY, C/C	800/622-2686
Harpers Ferry, WV, National Park Service	304/535-6115
Hoboken, NJ, Cultural Affairs Coordinator	201/420-2207
Hopland, CA, Thatcher Inn	707/744-1890
Imperial Beach, CA, C/C	619/424-3151
Jerome, AZ, C/C	602/634-2900
Key West, FL, C/C	305/294-2587
Las Vegas, NV, "Hard-Core," CCVB	702/892-0711
Lily Dale, NY	communicate thru medium
Lopez Island, WA, C/C	206/468-3663
LA Conner C/C	206/466-4778
Los Angeles, CA, Downtown, CCVB	213/728-7222
Love Canal, NY, Greater Buffalo CCVB	800/BUFFALO
Niagara Falls CCVB	716/285-2400
Madawaska, ME, C/C	207/728-7000
Mission District, San Francisco, CA, C/C	415/391-2000
New Orleans, LA, Tourist & Convention Comm	504/566-5011
New Paltz, NY, C/C	914/255-0243
New York, NY (Notsosoho & South Bronx), CCVB	212/397-8222
New York Mills, MN, Cultural Center	218/385-3339
Nome, AK, CCVB	907/443-5535

Ocracoke, NC, Visitors Center 919/928-4531
Park City, UT, CCVB 801/649-6100
Portland, OR, Visitors Association 800/962-3700
Rogers Park, Chicago, IL, Chi. Off. of Tourism 312/280-5740
Royal Oak, MI, C/C 810/547-4000
Sandy Hook, NJ, National Park Service 908/872-0115
Santa Fe, NM, CCVB 800/777-2489
Seaside, FL, Community Development Corp. 904/231-4224
Seattle, WA, "Cafe Theme Park," CCVB 206/461-5840
Susquehanna Islands, PA,
    Harrisburg Tourism & Convention Bureau 800/995-0969
Taos, NM, C/C 800/732-8267
Takoma Park, MD, City Government 301/270-1700
    (in this participatory democracy, many events are organized by
    volunteers who use their home phones)
Upcountry/Paia, Maui, HI, C/C 808/871-7711
Venice, CA, CCVB 310/827-2366
Ward, CO, City Clerk, PO Box 149, Ward, CO 80481 .. no phone
West Berkeley, CA, Berkeley CCVB 800/847-4823
Wheeling, WV, CCVB 800/828-3097
Yellow Springs, OH, C/C 513/767-2686

ALTERNATIVE RADIO DIRECTORY
Selected stations with alternative or eclectic programming.

Adams-Morgan, Washington, DC
WAMU-FM, 88.5, National Public Radio (NPR), talk/bluegrass/eclectic
WPFW-FM, 89.3, Pacifica, jazz/international/talk
WDCU-FM, 90.1, Univ. of the District of Columbia, jazz/talk
Arcata, CA
KHSU-FM 90.5, NPR, Humboldt State University
Austin, TX
KGSR-FM 107.1, alternative
KVRX-FM 91.7, alternative, University of Texas
Clarksdale, MS
WROX-AM 1450, talk/blues, 80% local
Down-and-out Cambridge, MA
WHRB-FM 95.3
Downtown Los Angeles, CA
KPFK-FM 90.7, Pacifica
KCRW-FM 89.9, NPR, eclectic
KXLU-FM 88.9, NPR, alternative/classical/jazz
El Paso, TX,
KTEP-FM 88.5, NPR, jazz/classical/eclectic

Gaithersburg, MD, see **Adams-Morgan**
Key West, FL
WKRY-FM 93.5, jazz/classical/contemporary
Mission District, San Francisco, CA
KQED-FM 88.5, NPR
KUSF-FM 90.3, eclectic/alternative
KITS-FM 105.3, alternative
KEST-AM 1450, independent/new age
New Orleans, LA
WWNO-FM 89.9, NPR, classical/jazz/news, 47% local
WTUL-FM 91.5, NPR, independent
New Paltz, NY
WFNP-FM-88.7, NPR, State University of New York
Notsosoho, NY
WBAI-FM 95.5, Pacifica, eclectic
WKCR-FM 89.9, Columbia University, 100%1ocal, jazz/ethnic/blue-
    grass/classical/alternative
WNYC-AM 820, NPR, information
Portland, OR
KBPS-FM 89.9 (AM 1450), NPR, eclectic/educational
Rogers Park, Chicago, IL
WBEZ-FM 91.5, NPR, eclectic/talk/jazz
Santa Fe, NM
KIOT-FM 102.3, blues/jazz/hispanic/new age
South Bronx, NY, see **Notsosoho**
Takoma Park, MD, see **Adams-Morgan**
Venice, CA, see **Downtown L.A.**
West Berkeley, CA
KPFA-FM 94.1, Pacifica, 98% local/alternative
KBLX-FM 102.9 (also AM 1400), jazz/alternative/independent
KALX-FM 90.7, alternative/eclectic
Yellow Springs, OH
WYSO-FM 91.3, NPR, 72% local

BIZARRE ANNUAL EVENT DIRECTORY

Selected events: although we emphasize places that celebrate daily existence, various annual events that transcend typical festivals are listed here.

January
Cowboy Poetry Gathering, Elko, NV
Sundance Film Festival, Park City, UT

February
Mardi Gras, Tues. before Ash Weds, New Orleans, LA (sometimes falls in March)
March
Bering Sea Ice Golf Classic, closest Sunday to St. Patrick's Day Nome, AK
Iditarod, Nome, AK
April
Smelt fishing, a month, Apr-May, Rogers Park, Chicago, IL
Conference of UFO Investigators, Eureka Springs, AR
Jazz & Heritage Festival, last weekend in April through first weekend in May, New Orleans, LA
May
Spring Art Festival, May-June, Taos, NM
Carnaval, Memorial Day, Mission District, San Francisco, CA
Venice Art Walk, Venice, CA
Kinetic Sculpture Race, Memorial Day, Arcata, CA
Crawfish Festival, first weekend in May, Breaux Bridge, LA
June
Acadian Festival, late June, Madawaska, ME
Music in the mountains, all summer, daily, Park City, UT
Native American Pow Wow, Delta Park, Portland, OR
Great American Think-off, New York Mills, MN
July
Basque Festival, July 4th weekend, Elko, NV
Oregon Brewers Festival, McCall Waterfront, Portland, OR
Taos Pueblo Pow Wow, Taos, NM
International Sand Castle Competition, Imperial Beach, CA
Continental Divide Music and Film Festival, New York Mills, MN
August
Sunflower River Blues Festival, early Aug, Clarksdale, MS
International Day, Adams-Morgan, DC
Annual Bat Migration, Congress Avenue Bridge, Austin, TX
Mendocino Bounty, Gourmet Food & Wine Festival, Hopland, CA
September
Artquake, Pioneer Square, Portland, OR
Fall Art Festival, Sept.-Oct., Taos, NM
Adams-Morgan Day, Adams-Morgan, DC
Bathtub Race, Labor Day, Nome, AK
All-Species Parade, North Country Fair, Arcata, CA
October
Tennessee Williams Festival, mid-Oct, Clarksdale, MS
December
Midnight Sun Festival, Nome, AK

PRESERVATION AND RESTORATION SITES

Alcazar Hotel, Clarksdale
Art Deco, Grand Concourse, South Bronx
Art Deco, Greyhound Station, Clarksdale
Bradbury Building, Los Angeles
Capitol Music Hall, Wheeling
Chassman & Bem Bookstore (opera house), Burlington
Churchill Weavers, Berea
Citadel (Uniroyal Tire & Rubber Factory)
Clifton's Cafeteria, Los Angeles
Clocktower Apartments, Hoboken
Columbus Historical Museum (Pancho Villa)
Customs House, Columbus
Dolores Mission, San Francisco
Eureka Ghost Town, Ely
Grand Central Market, Los Angeles
Harpers Ferry National Park
Historic Walks, Cambridge
House and Garden Tours, Takoma Park
Jacoby's Storehouse, Arcata
Jerome House Tours
LA Conner, town policy
Liberty Center for the Performing Arts, Eunice
Lily Dale Community Club
M-Zone, West Berkeley
Million Dollar Theatre, Los Angeles
Minor Theatre, Arcata
New York Mills Regional Cultural Center
Olde Towne Tavern & Brewing Co., Gaithersburg
Palace of the Governors, Santa Fe
Pennsylvania State Capitol, Harrisburg
Park City, downtown
Riverside Hotel (Bessie Smith), Clarksdale
Rockville Bridge, Susquehanna River
San Francisco de Asis, Taos
Sandy Hook Lighthouse
Skidmore Historic District, Portland
South Bronx Historic Districts
Star Hotel, Elko
Taos Pueblo
Telescope, Elko
Thatcher Hotel, Hopland,
Ward Charcoal Ovens, Ely
Warehouse District, New Orleans
Waterfront Warehouses, Burlington
Ye Olde Trail Tavern & Restaurant, Yellow Springs